CUBA
GOODING JR.

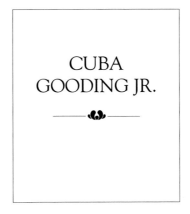

CUBA GOODING JR.

Paula Edelson

CHELSEA HOUSE PUBLISHERS
Philadelphia

Chelsea House Publishers

Editor in Chief	Stephen Reginald
Production Manager	Pamela Loos
Art Director	Sara Davis
Director of Photography	Judy L. Hasday
Managing Editor	James D. Gallagher
Senior Production Editor	J. Christopher Higgins

Staff for CUBA GOODING JR.

Associate Art Director	Takeshi Takahashi
Design & Production	21st Century Publishing and Communications
Cover Designer	Keith Trego
Cover photos	Sean Roberts/The Everett Collection

The Chelsea House World Wide Web address is
http://www.chelseahouse.com

First Printing

1 3 5 7 9 8 6 4 2

Library of Congress Cataloging-in-Publication Data

applied for
ISBN 0-7910-5275-3 (hc)
     0-7910-5276-1 (pb)

Frontispiece:
A talented actor with a dynamic screen presence, Cuba Gooding Jr. is one of Hollywood's rising young stars.

CONTENTS

BLACK AMERICANS OF ACHIEVEMENT

❧

HENRY AARON
baseball great

KAREEM ABDUL-JABBAR
basketball great

MUHAMMAD ALI
heavyweight champion

RICHARD ALLEN
religious leader and social activist

MAYA ANGELOU
author

LOUIS ARMSTRONG
musician

ARTHUR ASHE
tennis great

JOSEPHINE BAKER
entertainer

JAMES BALDWIN
author

TYRA BANKS
model

BENJAMIN BANNEKER
scientist and mathematician

COUNT BASIE
bandleader and composer

ANGELA BASSETT
actress

ROMARE BEARDEN
artist

HALLE BERRY
actress

MARY McLEOD BETHUNE
educator

GEORGE WASHINGTON
CARVER
botanist

JOHNNIE COCHRAN
lawyer

SEAN "PUFFY" COMBS
music producer

BILL COSBY
entertainer

MILES DAVIS
musician

FREDERICK DOUGLASS
abolitionist editor

CHARLES DREW
physician

W. E. B. DU BOIS
scholar and activist

PAUL LAURENCE DUNBAR
poet

DUKE ELLINGTON
bandleader and composer

RALPH ELLISON
author

JULIUS ERVING
basketball great

LOUIS FARRAKHAN
political activist

ELLA FITZGERALD
singer

ARETHA FRANKLIN
entertainer

MORGAN FREEMAN
actor

MARCUS GARVEY
black nationalist leader

JOSH GIBSON
baseball great

WHOOPI GOLDBERG
entertainer

CUBA GOODING JR.
actor

ALEX HALEY
author

PRINCE HALL
social reformer

JIMI HENDRIX
musician

MATTHEW HENSON
explorer

GREGORY HINES
performer

BILLIE HOLIDAY
singer

LENA HORNE
entertainer

WHITNEY HOUSTON
singer and actress

LANGSTON HUGHES
poet

JANET JACKSON
musician

JESSE JACKSON
civil-rights leader and politician

MICHAEL JACKSON
entertainer

SAMUEL L. JACKSON *actor*	JOE LOUIS *heavyweight champion*	ROSA PARKS *civil-rights leader*	TINA TURNER *entertainer*
T. D. JAKES *religious leader*	RONALD MCNAIR *astronaut*	COLIN POWELL *military leader*	ALICE WALKER *author*
JACK JOHNSON *heavyweight champion*	MALCOLM X *militant black leader*	PAUL ROBESON *singer and actor*	MADAM C. J. WALKER *entrepreneur*
MAGIC JOHNSON *basketball great*	BOB MARLEY *musician*	JACKIE ROBINSON *baseball great*	BOOKER T. WASHINGTON *educator*
SCOTT JOPLIN *composer*	THURGOOD MARSHALL *Supreme Court justice*	CHRIS ROCK *comedian and actor*	DENZEL WASHINGTON *actor*
BARBARA JORDAN *politician*	TERRY MCMILLAN *author*	DIANA ROSS *entertainer*	J. C. WATTS *politician*
MICHAEL JORDAN *basketball great*	TONI MORRISON *author*	WILL SMITH *actor*	VANESSA WILLIAMS *singer and actress*
CORETTA SCOTT KING *civil-rights leader*	ELIJAH MUHAMMAD *religious leader*	WESLEY SNIPES *actor*	OPRAH WINFREY *entertainer*
MARTIN LUTHER KING, JR. *civil-rights leader*	EDDIE MURPHY *entertainer*	CLARENCE THOMAS *Supreme Court justice*	TIGER WOODS *golf star*
LEWIS LATIMER *scientist*	JESSE OWENS *champion athlete*	SOJOURNER TRUTH *antislavery activist*	RICHARD WRIGHT *author*
SPIKE LEE *filmmaker*	SATCHEL PAIGE *baseball great*	HARRIET TUBMAN *antislavery activist*	
CARL LEWIS *champion athlete*	CHARLIE PARKER *musician*	NAT TURNER *slave revolt leader*	

ON
ACHIEVEMENT

———— ❦ ————

Coretta Scott King

Before you begin this book, I hope you will ask yourself what the word *excellence* means to you. I think it's a question we should all ask, and keep asking as we grow older and change. Because the truest answer to it should never change. When you think of excellence, perhaps you think of success at work; or of becoming wealthy; or meeting the right person, getting married, and having a good family life.

Those goals are worth striving for, but there is a better way to look at excellence. As Martin Luther King Jr. said in one of his last sermons, "I want you to be first in love. I want you to be first in moral excellence. I want you to be first in generosity. If you want to be important, wonderful. If you want to be great, wonderful. But recognize that he who is greatest among you shall be your servant."

My husband knew that the true meaning of achievement is service. When I met him, in 1952, he was already ordained as a Baptist minister and was working toward a doctoral degree at Boston University. I was studying at the New England Conservatory and dreamed of accomplishments in music. We married a year later, and after I graduated the following year we moved to Montgomery, Alabama. We didn't know it then, but our notions of achievement were about to undergo a dramatic change.

You may have read or heard about what happened next. What began with the boycott of a local bus line grew into a national crusade, and by the time he was assassinated in 1968 my husband had fashioned a black movement powerful enough to shatter forever the practice of racial segregation. What you may not have read about is where he learned to resist injustice without compromising his religious beliefs.

He adopted a strategy of nonviolence from a man of a different race, who lived in a different country and even practiced a different religion. The man was Mahatma Gandhi, the great leader of India, who devoted his life to serving humanity in the spirit of love and nonviolence. It was in these principles that Martin discovered his method for social reform. More than anything else, those two principles were the key to his achievements.

These books are about African Americans who served society through the excellence of their achievements. They form part of the rich history of black men and women in America—a history of stunning accomplishments in every field of human endeavor, from literature and art to science, industry, education, diplomacy, athletics, jurisprudence, even polar exploration.

Not all of the people in this history had the same ideals, but I think you will find that all of them had something in common. Like Martin Luther King Jr., they all decided to become "drum majors" and serve humanity. In that principle—whether it was expressed in books, inventions, or song—they found a goal and a guide outside themselves that showed them a way to serve others instead of living only for themselves.

Reading the stories of these courageous men and women not only helps us discover the principles that we will use to guide our own lives; it also teaches us about our black heritage and about America itself. It is crucial for us to know the heroes and heroines of our history and to realize that the price we paid in our struggle for equality in America was dear. But we must also understand that we have gotten as far as we have partly because America's democratic system and ideals made it possible.

We are still struggling with racism and prejudice. But the great men and women in this series are a tribute to the spirit of the country in which they have flourished. And that makes their stories special and worth knowing.

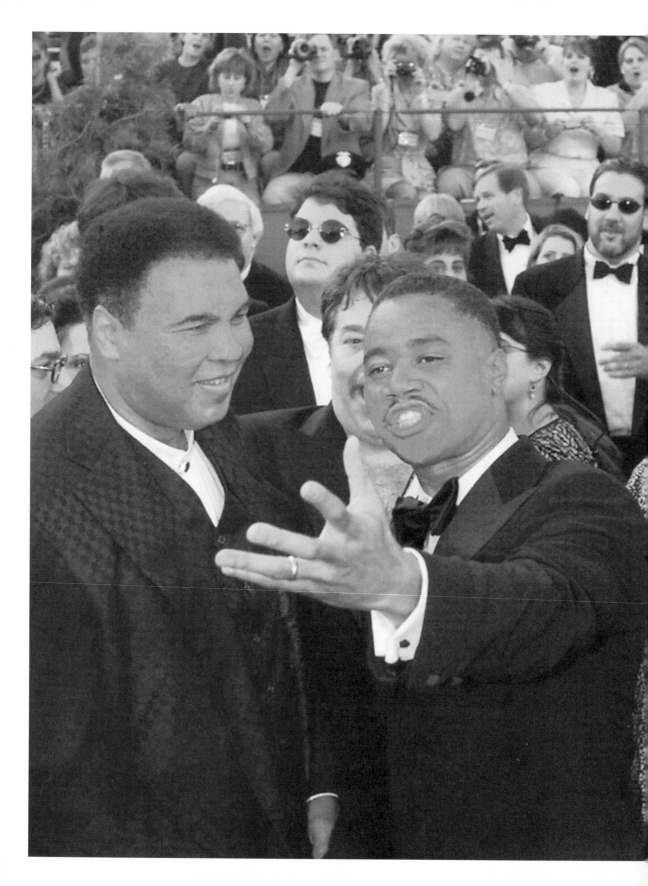

1

"THE OSCAR GOES TO . . ."

$\textit{Cuba Gooding Jr. has the attention of boxing great Muhammad Ali (left) as they arrive at the 1997 Academy Awards. When Cuba won the award as Best Supporting Actor, he was only the sixth African American in the 69-year history of the awards to take home an Oscar.}$

ON MARCH 24, 1997, five men seated in Hollywood's Dorothy Chandler Pavilion fidgeted nervously. They were part of the well-dressed crowd attending the 69th Academy Awards ceremony as the first award was about to be presented. The gathering of Hollywood's brightest stars—and a television audience of millions—anxiously waited to hear who would win the Oscar for best performance by an actor in a supporting role. Mira Sorvino, the gifted actress presenting the award, read the names of the five finalists. "Cuba Gooding Jr. for *Jerry Maguire*; William H. Macy for *Fargo*; Armin Mueller-Stahl for *Shine*; Edward Norton for *Primal Fear*; and James Woods for *Ghosts of Mississippi*."

Every year the film industry's elite gathers for the Academy Awards, a lavish ceremony that recognizes the finest cinematic achievements of the previous year. For those in the motion picture business, the Academy Awards are the most important event of the year. Winning an Oscar is arguably the pinnacle of achievement for any actor, director, producer, or screenwriter. Even for those nominees who don't win one of the small gold statuettes, simply being nominated is an honor of the highest order.

The Academy Awards broadcast is also one of the highlights of the year for movie fans. Every year countless viewers around the world watch the presentation of the Oscars. A live (and often exceedingly long) tele-cast noted for its high glamour quotient and scrutinized for weeks after its airing, the Academy Awards show has become an instantly recognizable institution of contemporary American culture.

The selection of Cuba Gooding Jr. as one of the five contenders for a best supporting actor award was unusual, in light of the history of the Oscars. Before Cuba Gooding's tense night at the Dorothy Chandler Pavilion, only five African Americans had actually taken home Oscars for acting performances. The first of these winners, Hattie McDaniel, had won her award for best performance in a supporting role for her part as Mammie, a southern slave during the Civil War, in the 1939 classic *Gone With The Wind*. Although McDaniel was invited to attend the Academy Awards ceremony in the spring of 1940, a policy of segregating whites and blacks required her to sit in the back of the auditorium for the evening.

In 1996 the Reverend Jesse Jackson, one of America's most passionate African-American activists, had called upon African Americans across the nation to picket TV stations carrying the 68th Academy Awards broadcast (which recognized the cinematic achievements of the preceding year, 1995) to protest the dearth of black nominees. Only one of the 166 nominees that year was an African American—Dianne Houston, who had directed a live short-subject piece called *Tuesday Morning Ride*. She did not win. Many talented black actors who had deliv-ered noteworthy performances in films during 1995 had been left off the list of 1996 Oscar finalists. Among them were Laurence Fishburne and Denzel Washington, both of whom had received Oscar nominations in previous years. (Washington had, in fact, won an Academy Award in 1990 for his sup-porting role in *Glory*.)

In 1997, fifty-seven years after McDaniel's groundbreaking victory, the climate at the Academy

The first African American to win an Academy Award, veteran actor Hattie McDaniel had appeared in numerous films before she received an Oscar. Although admired in the film world for her talents, when she died in 1952 she was refused burial at the Hollywood Memorial Park Cemetery because she was black.

Awards had vastly improved for African Americans. But it was clear that tremendous inequities still remained. That year, studies examining racial balances in the film industry uncovered some disturbing facts. For example, although African Americans are the largest minority group in the United States—comprising 12 percent of the American public—this is not reflected in the membership of the Academy of Motion Picture Arts and Sciences. African Americans represent just four percent of this group, which is responsible for selecting Oscar nominees and electing the winners.

At the 1996 Academy Awards ceremony, which took place on March 24, 1997, there were just two African-American nominees in the acting categories.

As director of the live-action short-subject film, Tuesday Morning Ride, *Diane Houston was the single black nominee on the 1996 Academy Awards list. The omission of several black actors who had turned in sterling performances that year brought protest from African-American activists.*

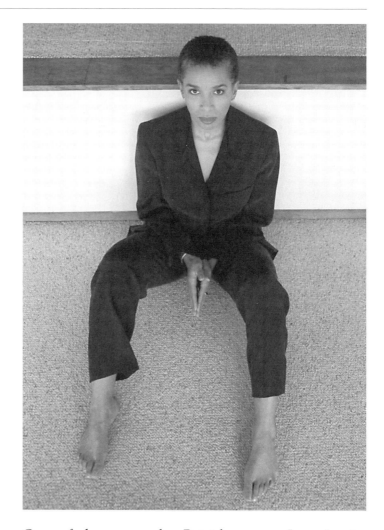

One of them was the British actress Jean Louis-Baptiste, who was nominated for Best Actress for her role in *Secrets and Lies*. The other was Cuba Gooding Jr., who was chosen as one of the five Best Supporting Actor nominees for his high-powered portrayal of football player Rod Tidwell in the hit movie *Jerry Maguire*.

Just 29 years old at the time, Gooding was not an established Hollywood star. In fact, not many people outside of the industry had heard of the young actor before the release of *Jerry Maguire*. Most movie fans assumed that Cuba Gooding Jr. was an overnight success, but people who knew the actor—a veteran of some 11 movies at the time of his Oscar nomination—knew that Gooding's journey to this night at the Dorothy Chandler Pavilion had not been an easy one. He had overcome a difficult childhood, during which he had taken a number of menial jobs to help support his mother, brother, and sister. Gooding Jr.'s first break came in 1984, when the 16-year-old performed a break-dancing routine at the closing ceremonies of the Los Angeles Summer Olympic games. He later landed roles in commercials and some small parts in television series.

In 1991, Gooding exploded onto the movie scene with his stunning performance as Tre Styles, a 17-year-old caught between the responsibilities of non-violent manhood and the lure of gang warfare on the streets of Los Angeles in the John Singleton film *Boyz N the Hood*. Critics noted his talent and predicted a great future for the then 21-year-old actor. But after that role, Gooding's career stalled. The movies he starred in didn't do well critically or commercially, and his few big-budget film appearances were in very small roles. By 1995, Cuba Gooding Jr. had been all but forgotten by the Hollywood community.

Then Gooding landed the part of Rod Tidwell in *Jerry Maguire*. Playing a cocky and energetic football player, Gooding appeared opposite Tom Cruise, who portrayed a sports agent who faces a crisis of conscience. Gooding's performance won raves from critics and audiences alike. It had also netted him a Golden Globe Award for best supporting actor earlier in 1997. But the most significant honor for Gooding was his Oscar nomination. It carried a special significance not only for Gooding himself but also for the entire African-American film community. Many believed that if he won, the victory would help advance the standing of his race, which was underrepresented and underappreciated in Hollywood.

Cuba reacted exuberantly on the stage as the audience cheered his Oscar win. Raising his trophy high into the air in triumph and leaping for joy, he enthusiastically performed his victory dance.

But if Cuba Gooding Jr. felt the hopes of an entire race resting on his young shoulders, it wasn't apparent at the Academy Awards ceremony. Seated with his wife and his *Jerry Maguire* costars, he leaned forward excitedly as Mira Sorvino read the names of each nominated actor, and a short clip of each performance was shown. At last, Sorvino opened a sealed envelope. "And the Oscar goes to . . . Cuba Gooding Jr. for *Jerry Maguire*!" she announced.

As the crowd exploded into cheers and applause, Gooding hugged his wife and bounded up the aisle and onto the stage. He took his Oscar, turned to the enthusiastic crowd, and excitedly thanked everyone near and dear to him, both on and off screen. "My wife, I love you! My children, my parents, I love you!

Tom Cruise, I love you man!" Gooding cried. He was clearly in no hurry to leave the stage. Oscar winners are normally allotted 30 seconds for their acceptance speeches. Gooding's half-minute sped by, but he wasn't finished yet. As music played to signal that his speaking time was over, Gooding raised his voice to be heard above it. "Okay, here we go!" he shouted. Gooding then kept going, expressing his gratitude and excitement until he was finished. Then with a broad smile and with arms raised triumphantly, he took his Oscar and walked happily backstage to greet reporters and photographers.

So exuberant was Gooding's acceptance that host Billy Crystal joked, "If there is anyone who has not been thanked by Cuba, please give me your name. He's waiting backstage."

Gooding's speech may well have been one of the most moving in the history of the Oscars. Rather than speaking of politics or of his personal struggles, he chose to express his sincere joy and true delight in being honored by his peers. It was a speech Rod Tidwell, Gooding's scene-stealing alter ego in *Jerry Maguire*, would have been proud to deliver.

Honored with his industry's highest award, Cuba Gooding Jr. had truly arrived in Hollywood.

2

EARLY DAYS

✿

Although Cuba Gooding Jr. came of age during an era of abundant media attention for celebrities, little information is available about his life. This is not accidental because Gooding is intensely private. He protects his personal life and chooses to say little to the press about his family.

It is known that he was born in New York City on January 2, 1968, to Cuba Gooding Sr., a professional singer, and his wife, Shirley, a homemaker (and former backup singer). Cuba Jr. was one of three children: he has a younger brother named Omar (who is also an actor) and a younger sister named April. The Goodings lived in the Bronx district of New York City during Cuba Jr.'s early childhood.

While Cuba is named for his father, the name originated with Cuba Jr.'s grandfather. "My grandfather, whose name was Dudley, was a sea merchant," Cuba later explained. "He was from Cuba. When he moved to the States, he became a taxicab driver in Manhattan. His nickname was Cuba. He named my father Cuba. So I'm unofficially the third."

In the early 1970s, Cuba Gooding Sr.'s rhythm-and-blues group, The Main Ingredient, recorded such chart-topping hits as "Just Don't Want to Be Lonely" and "Everybody Plays the Fool." The latter song, a 1972 smash, enabled the elder Gooding to move his young family out of the Bronx and into sun-drenched

Cuba shares the spotlight with his mother. As a teenager, he struggled to keep his family together through lean years by taking odd jobs. He finally broke into show business with supporting roles on television.

As a successful singer, Cuba Gooding Sr. kept his family in luxury for a time. When he left, however, Cuba and his siblings quickly went from riches to rags.

southern California. For a time, the Goodings lived in style.

But life for Cuba and his siblings soon changed dramatically. His parents split up and his father left the family in 1974. Suddenly Cuba and his siblings, who had once known luxury, were thrust into a world of poverty. His family began moving from home to home: they were evicted for missing rent payments on more than one occasion. At one point, the family even lived in the desert in their car.

Money was scarce. The family lived on welfare for a while, with Cuba and his siblings frequently taking odd jobs in order to help provide for the household. "All of this happened before I was 16," Gooding later told *Scholastic Update* magazine. "I would go out and pull weeds, wash cars, do the paperboy route, anything to make ends meet so I could come home with food for the table at the end of the day." Those years were financially difficult for his family, but Gooding never shirked his obligations or abandoned the people he loved.

Although he was busy working to help keep his family afloat, he was also becoming interested in performing. That urge to perform initially came through in the midst of a dance craze that swept across America during the early 1980s. Break dancing emerged along with the new, urban sounds of rap music. Break dancing was so named because during breaks in the music at parties and rap concerts, dancers would do the moonwalk, head spins, and other athletic moves.

Gooding credits break dancing with helping him stay out of trouble. Minority youths in urban neighborhoods often face pressure to join the world of gangs and drugs. Gooding knows he was fortunate that he did not become involved with either. "That background [Los Angeles] is where I was exposed to kids like the characters in *Boyz N the Hood*," he told the *Chicago Tribune*. "But I met up with some other kids who were break dancers, and I started spinning on my head, channeling my energy into that."

Gooding also managed to stay in school and keep up with his studies. "At one point in my life, I was getting on a bus at 6 in the morning, at school by 7:30, doing my homework for about 45 minutes before school started, and going until 3," he told *American Visions* magazine. "I did a couple more hours of homework on the bus going to work, and then I worked from 5 to 11." Cuba often didn't arrive home until one o'clock in the morning for a brief night's sleep before heading off to school again a few hours later. Cuba was liked and respected by his classmates. According to an online biography of

Cuba shows off some dance
steps to a crowd. While he
was a teenager, Cuba got his
opening into show business
through his break dancing.
His performances, as well as
his roles in high school plays,
attracted the attention of
agents and started him on
his way to an acting career.

Gooding at the *MovieThing* website, he attended four
different high schools and was elected class president
at three of them.

It was during his high school years that Cuba
became interested in acting. In fact, as a senior, he
won top honors in a Shakespeare competition.
Gooding later recalled that his performance in that
contest wasn't a dramatic reading, but a hilarious—
and wordless—interpretation of a scene from *Twelfth
Night*. "I incorporated a lot of pantomime into
explaining things I didn't understand," Gooding

later said of his first acting triumph in an interview with *Scholastic Update* magazine. "The physical comedy got me over."

During high school, Cuba began dating Sara Kapfer, the young woman he would eventually marry. "We've been together since 1986," Gooding has said of his relationship with Sara. "I graduated in 1986 and she graduated in 1988. We began dating when she was 17." Cuba and Sara married in 1994, and the couple has two sons.

It was while he was in high school that Cuba also got his first real break in show business. He was living in a motel room with his family at the time. Cuba and some friends from the same motel would get together every day to practice and perform break-dancing routines that they had choreographed themselves. One day an agent who happened to catch their act asked Cuba and his friends if they were interested in break dancing at the closing ceremonies for the 1984 Olympic Games, which were being held in Los Angeles. Cuba ended up dancing while Lionel Ritchie, a popular singer/songwriter who had scored hits such as "Dancing on the Ceiling" and "Penny Lover" in the early 1980s, sang at the Olympic closing. After the Games, an agent spotted Cuba performing in a high school play and signed him. He then started auditioning for acting roles.

His early efforts were not wildly successful, however. Cuba landed a few commercials and played some minor parts in television programs. But those early years also included many rejections. Ironically, Gooding, who had won his high school Shakespeare contest on the basis of his flair for physical comedy, could not win roles on TV comedy programs, except for a 1986 appearance on the Sherman Hemsley sitcom *Amen*. It certainly wasn't for lack of trying, though. "Anytime I was put on the spot to do something funny," he told *Scholastic Update*, "it never really worked out."

It finally dawned on Gooding that maybe the best road to acting success would be the one he had traveled in real life. He started incorporating his difficult childhood experiences into his acting and began auditioning for dramatic parts. Almost immediately, he was cast in TV roles that kept food on the table but left him uncomfortable. He played a drug pusher on *Hill Street Blues*, and landed a regular guest-starring role on *MacGyver* as a bounty hunter.

The parts he played were hardly glamorous, but they did pay Gooding's bills. "Those roles were rotten," he told *Scholastic Update*. "But the reality is that you've got to eat."

Gooding was also cast in the 1988 Eddie Murphy film *Coming to America*, though most of his comedic turn as a customer in a barbershop ended up on the cutting room floor. The next year he appeared in another film. *Sing*, a musical directed by Richard Baskin, was about a talent contest at a Brooklyn high school. While he was on-screen longer in *Sing* than he had been in *Coming to America*, the movie was not a hit with critics. One reviewer described *Sing's* plot as "a thin excuse for endless musical numbers, none believable in the supposedly realistic context of the film."

All this time, the young actor dreamed of a quality role that would stretch his talents. "I've played all sorts of roles, from a street hoodlum to a cop," Gooding later told the *Chicago Tribune*. "I don't mind playing a bad guy if the work itself brings forth a positive message. But the heroic, positive image is really addictive."

But although Gooding wished for better parts, his early television and movie roles—and indeed, the early years of struggle that laid the foundation for his future performances—did more than put food on Gooding's table. They also turned the head of a young filmmaker looking for gutsy actors who could credibly play gritty roles. That filmmaker, John Singleton, had

Cuba (in the front) poses with the cast of the TV program MacGyver, on which he appeared from 1989 to 1991. His early efforts were not very successful. Describing some of these roles as "rotten," he was determined to find roles in which he could express a positive image.

been impressed by Cuba Gooding Jr.'s work in *Coming to America* and in otherwise forgettable television programs. He asked the young actor to audition for the leading role in his new movie. That film, which would turn out to be a dramatically honest and forthright account of life on the streets of Los Angeles, was called *Boyz N the Hood*.

3

Boyz N the Hood

———— ✿ ————

Most movie buffs identify Cuba Gooding Jr. with his Oscar-winning turn as Rod Tidwell, the football player who teaches his agent a thing or two about life and love in the 1996 movie *Jerry Maguire*. Gooding gave a memorable performance as Tidwell, and his Academy Award was richly deserved. Moreover, *Jerry Maguire* was a great success with movie critics and fans alike.

Even so, perhaps Cuba Gooding Jr.'s most important movie is the 1991 John Singleton film *Boyz N the Hood*. His portrayal of Tre Styles established Gooding as a promising young on-screen presence. After his minor roles in *Coming to America* and *Sing*, Gooding clearly needed a vehicle that would showcase his talent for a larger audience. *Boyz N the Hood* did just that—and more. The movie set a new standard for realism in portraying life in an African-American ghetto, and it awakened the nation to some very real problems brewing in America's inner cities.

Boyz N the Hood wastes no time in making a statement. As the movie begins, words on the screen inform the viewer that homicide is the leading cause of death among young African-American males, and that most of these murder victims are killed by other young African-American men. This endless cycle of genocidal violence forms a backdrop for all the

In Boyz N the Hood, *his first major role, Cuba's sensitive portrayal of a young black man caught in the violence and hopelessness of the ghetto won him acclaim and a promising acting career.*

relationships among the characters in the film.

"*Boyz N the Hood* could easily be dismissed by cynics—in particular those who haven't seen it—as just another angry black film finding its way into theaters on the heels of Spike Lee's mainstream studio-backed success," Chris Hicks wrote in his review of *Boyz* for the Deseret News Service. "And the cynic in me does see that as part of the reason Columbia Pictures picked up this low-budget, independent picture."

Hicks, who goes on to emphasize that *Boyz* is in fact a "more thoughtful than angry" film, was contrasting it with the work of Spike Lee, a talented African-American filmmaker. Perhaps Lee's most celebrated and critically successful movie was the 1989 film *Do the Right Thing*. Set in Brooklyn's seedier neighborhoods in the heat of midsummer, *Do the Right Thing* clearly depicted racial tension and the seemingly ever-present potential for violence in a poor urban area. The climactic scene of *Do the Right Thing*—in which a pizza parlor owned by Italian Americans is broken into and looted by a group of angry African Americans—was unsettling to some viewers who found the scene's violence to be gratuitous and overly graphic.

But if *Do the Right Thing* struck some moviegoers as unnecessarily violent, others might have seen it as a wake-up call. In truth, racial tensions, poverty, and hopelessness had already combined to make violence a fact of life in the inner city, as two real-life incidents would prove in 1991.

The first of these incidents began brewing one night in March 1991 in Los Angeles. An African-American motorist named Rodney King was pulled over by police. When King got out of his car, the police beat him severely, leaving him injured and barely conscious. Unbeknownst to police, however, a man who lived near the scene of the incident was trying out his new video camera, and he taped the

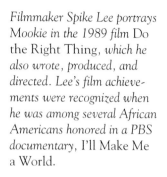

Filmmaker Spike Lee portrays Mookie in the 1989 film Do the Right Thing, *which he also wrote, produced, and directed. Lee's film achievements were recognized when he was among several African Americans honored in a PBS documentary,* I'll Make Me a World.

beating. This amateur videographer released the tape to the media. A now-infamous segment of that tape showed that King was unarmed, and that he did not retaliate as the police beat him. People of all races were horrified by the footage; the four police officers involved in the beating were indicted on charges of assault and battery.

Ten months later, an all-white jury acquitted three of the accused officers. All charges against Sergeant Stacey Koon, Officer Timothy Wind, and Officer Theodore Briseno were dropped, but the jury failed to reach a verdict on the charge that Officer Lawrence Powell had used excessive force under color of authority. Several months later, however, Powell was convicted on that charge and sentenced to probation.

Although the sentence seemed shamefully lenient to many Americans, the very videotape that had gotten the officers into trouble also contained exculpatory evidence. Television stations around the country had aired only one portion of the videotape, which showed Rodney King as the passive victim of a beating by Los Angeles police officers. But there was another portion of the tape that that TV broadcasts didn't show: an earlier segment showing King charging and attacking the police officers. The jury did see that part, however. On the basis of King's initial attack, the jury decided to acquit three of the four officers—despite the fact that King was unarmed and clearly outnumbered.

The not-guilty verdict was announced shortly before dusk on April 29, 1992. Many African Americans in the Los Angeles area were outraged by the verdict. They believed the jury's decision was racially motivated. They felt that if Rodney King had been a white man, he would never have received a brutal beating in the first place. They also believed that if the jury had not been all white, the police officers would have been convicted.

A mere three hours after the verdict, entire sections of Los Angeles were ablaze, while violence and looting went on unchecked. The Rodney King riots lasted for three days. By the time the rioting ended on the evening of May 1, 1992, 52 people had died.

Two years later the police officers were tried again, this time on federal charges. This time, two of the previously acquitted officers were found guilty of violating King's civil rights. The Rodney King incident proved to be a travesty for the Los Angeles police department, not only because of the King beating itself, but because the police failed to

anticipate or control the widespread violent expressions of outrage that occurred in the acquittal's aftermath.

Another episode of urban violence that gripped the nation also had its beginnings in 1991. The Crown Heights incident was touched off on the night of August 19, 1991, when a Hasidic Jewish motorist accidentally struck and killed a seven-year-old boy named Gavin Cato in the Crown Heights neighborhood of Brooklyn.

The child's death was clearly unintentional, yet some members of the African-American community

Police patrol the Crown Heights section of Brooklyn following the 1991 rioting that ended in the death of a young Hasidic man. Long before the riots erupted, the neighborhood had a history of uneasy coexistence between African Americans and Hasidic Jews.

were outraged because Gavin's killer faced no legal penalties. This anger led to three days and nights of rioting by some African Americans in Crown Heights. The riots culminated in the stabbing death of Yankel Rosenbaum, a young Jewish scholar. Rosenbaum's alleged killer was an African-American teenager named Lemrick Nelson.

In 1997, a federal jury found Nelson and another African American, Charles Price, guilty of violating Yankel Rosenbaum's civil rights. Rosenbaum had identified Nelson as his assailant before dying, but a state court had acquitted him of the actual murder. Price was also convicted on the federal charges because he had encouraged the rioting and incited the rioters to "get Jews." The city of New York eventually offered an apology to the Jewish community in Crown Heights for not offering sufficient police protection when the riots erupted.

John Singleton had made *Boyz N the Hood* before either the Rodney King or Crown Heights riots had taken place. Although *Boyz* focuses its attention on the problem of black-on-black violence, the fact that both of these real-life violent outbursts were ignited in the same year that Singleton's movie was released shows the filmmaker's acute awareness of just how real the problem of urban violence had become.

The movie opens in an elementary school classroom in Los Angeles. A white teacher is having trouble maintaining order in her class of mostly minority students. In frustration, she asks young Tre Styles (Desi Arnaz Hines), who is the main cause of the disruption, if he wants to teach the class. "Go ahead," she dares him. "See how easy it is." Tre shrugs his shoulders and says, "All right." He saunters up to the front of the classroom, takes a large pointer, and points out Africa on the world map hanging from the front of the blackboard. "See here, that's Africa," he tells the class. "That's where the first man and woman were born. Everyone in this room and in the world come from these two people. That means everyone in the world is first from Africa."

His classmates are fascinated by what Tre is saying, but not all of them agree with him. One boy tells Tre what he's saying isn't true and walks up to the front of the room to confront Tre. Tre starts yelling at the other boy and loses his temper, hitting the boy across the chest with the pointer. Tre is suspended, and when the teacher calls his mother, Reva (Angela Bassett), to talk to her about Tre's behavior problems, she makes a decision: Tre, who has been living with her all of his life, will now move in with his father. "Yes he has one," Reva tells the teacher over the phone. "What do you think, that we make them ourselves?"

Tre's mother, who is trying to get a master's degree in social work, tells Tre that she fears that she can't give him the discipline he needs to grow into a responsible adult. She's particularly concerned because in the impoverished part of Los Angeles in which both she and Tre's father live, it is all too easy to slip into an endless cycle of anger, violence, and murder. Tre's father, Furious Styles (Laurence Fishburne), dives right into full-time parenting, starting his son on a strict but loving regimen of chores, discipline, and father-son talks to mold the boy into a conscientious and upstanding young man.

Tre, who had regularly visited his father before moving in, is quite familiar with the neighborhood. He spends his free time with his three friends from the "hood." Chris is a small, rather slow-witted youngster who follows more than he leads. Doughboy, a heavyset child, means well but always manages to get into trouble. Doughboy's brother Ricky, rarely seen in the movie without a football in his hands, is a kindhearted, enthusiastic boy with dreams of one day playing in the NFL.

When we next see Tre, he is a 17-year-old high school senior, played by Cuba Gooding Jr. He has

With costars Laurence Fishburne (center) and Ice Cube (right), Cuba plays a scene from Boyz N the Hood. In his role as Tre Styles, who must make a choice between responsibility and succumbing to the brutality of the 'hood, Cuba was praised for his portrayal of a young man coming of age in the inner city.

grown up to become a responsible and thoughtful young man. Furious has obviously done a remarkable job. Tre has a job in a store and is fully intent on going to college after graduating from high school. The audience first sees Cuba's character at a barbecue dinner being held for Doughboy, who has become a sullen and defeated teenager, arrested and jailed on several occasions. Ricky, Tre's closest friend, is the star player for their high school football team, as well as the father of a young boy. Chris, the smallest member of the childhood foursome, is now in a wheelchair—the victim of a street-warfare shooting. Although Tre was the recipient of a much more disciplined upbringing than his other three friends, he is never condescending towards them. He talks trash with them, using their shared street language (which is liberally sprinkled with profanity). Tre also has a girlfriend, Brandi (Nia Long), to whom he is anxious to lose his virginity. (This was the first time Gooding shot a love scene; the young actor later characterized the experience as "hell" because he felt so awkward and uncomfortable.)

Gooding plays Tre in a subtle, understated manner. He manages to invest the character of Tre with a mixture of youthful naiveté and the cynicism of someone accustomed to seeing the uglier aspects of life on a daily basis. At one point in the film, he is walking down the street in his neighborhood when he hears a car horn blaring. Tre notices a toddler in the middle of the street. Rolling his eyes and shaking his head, Tre runs into the street, picks up the toddler, and waves the car on ahead. Tre carries the little girl home, rings the doorbell, and hands the child over to her mother. "Have any blow or rock?" asks the mother, craving a drug fix. "No," Tre answers. "Don't let your baby play in the street. And change her diaper—she smells bad—almost as bad as you." Gooding plays this scene matter-of-factly, making it clear that this kind of thing happens every day in Tre's world—and that even he has become so hardened to it that it no longer shocks him.

When the senseless violence and brutality of his neighborhood strike close enough to shatter Tre's world—one of his best friends is shot to death in front of him—he must decide whether or not to become violent himself. His choice will determine whether he becomes a successful man or just another faceless casualty of life in the 'hood.

The trouble begins one night as Ricky, Tre, Doughboy, Chris, and some of their other buddies are standing around talking at a street fair. When a group of young men strolls past, one walks menacingly up to Ricky and knocks him aside. Menacing stares are exchanged, and the two groups fire some insults at

In a dramatic scene in Boyz N the Hood, Tre wants to do the right thing and struggles to make a difficult choice. To make his character convincing, Cuba drew upon his own experiences as a young man in the ghetto.

one another before Doughboy jumps out of his car, pulls out a gun, and walks threateningly toward the other youths waving the weapon. The other group drives away, but it is clear that Ricky has been targeted for violence.

Ricky, Doughboy, Chris, and Tre resume their conversation, but they have been shaken by the confrontation—even more so when they hear shots being fired several minutes later. Several blocks away, Ricky's nemesis is shooting into the air, sending a message of fear to Ricky and his friends, who quickly leave the area.

Over the next few days, life continues as normal for Tre and his friends. Ricky is nervously awaiting the arrival of his SAT scores, worried that he won't meet the minimum requirement to qualify for a college football scholarship. As Ricky and Tre walk together, discussing their options, Tre spots a red car and recognizes the driver as the young man who had knocked Ricky aside at the fair. Sensing trouble, the two teens cut through an alley. The car swerves around a corner—the driver is looking for Ricky, and he has a gun. Doughboy and Chris, in the meantime, have also spotted the red car, and concerned for Ricky's life, they jump into Doughboy's car and rush to the scene.

Ricky and Trey, walking quietly in the alley in the hope that they have hidden successfully from Ricky's hunters, are trying to figure out the best and safest way to get home. "Let's split up," suggests Ricky, who is less concerned than Tre. "No way," Tre answers. "Better that we stick together." "No," says Ricky. "They're not looking for us anymore anyway." Tre worries, but he and Ricky decide to take separate routes and meet up at Ricky's house.

As Ricky walks down the alley, scratching at a lottery card, the red car suddenly pulls up. Tre spots the car first, and calls Ricky's name in desperation. His friend begins to run, but it's too late. The red car swerves behind him, and the front seat passenger sticks a gun out the window and shoots Ricky twice. Bleeding and twitching, Ricky falls to the ground. Tre gets there first and cradles his dying friend as Doughboy and Chris arrive on the scene.

Ricky's mother, his girlfriend, and their child are besides themselves in grief. With tears in her eyes Ricky's mother opens her son's SAT scores, which had arrived that morning, and sees that his scores were indeed high enough for him to have attended college. Bearing angry witness to their mourning is

Tre, who is clearly intent on seeking revenge. He plans to meet Doughboy and find his friend's killer, even though both Brandy and Furious try to talk him out of it. "You don't want to end up like them," Furious tells his son. "Like Doughboy, or in a wheelchair, like Chris." Tre has a lot to live for, his father says—don't risk it to settle a score.

Tre, however, refuses to listen. He joins Doughboy and Chris, searching for Ricky's killers. However, as they drive Tre is thinking about what he's doing, and eventually he asks to get out of the car.

Doughboy does find Ricky's killers that afternoon, and he shoots all four of the passengers in the red car. The next morning, Tre is sitting on his front stoop, eating some breakfast, when Doughboy comes over and tells his friend that he had been up early watching a program about how violent the world is. "It showed all these foreign places, man, where foreigners live," Doughboy says. "And I started thinking, either they don't know . . . or they don't care about what's happening in the 'hood. . . . All this stuff about other countries where foreigners live, and they didn't have nothing on my brother."

Doughboy and Tre embrace, and Doughboy walks slowly home. The movie ends with notes on each of the characters. Tre and Brandi each escape the neighborhood and attend predominantly African-American colleges in Atlanta. Doughboy, on the other hand, remains in the 'hood and watches his brother get buried. Two weeks later, Doughboy himself is shot and killed.

■   ■   ■

One of the reasons *Boyz* is such an extraordinary movie is because Singleton's script is not angry or bitter in tone; it is a straightforward and sympathetic story about coming of age in the inner city. Unlike other movies of its genre, the film does

not pontificate or take sides. Singleton had also assembled a great cast and elicited great performances from Fishburne, former rapper Ice Cube, Morris Chestnut, and up-and-coming actresses Nia Long and Angela Bassett, as well as from Cuba Gooding Jr.

Gooding's masterful performance put him on the Hollywood radar screen. He told *American Visions* magazine that he had drawn upon his own youthful experiences to make the character of Tre convincing. "I hung out with a lot of guys who ran in gangs," he said in a 1993 interview, "but I was never in one myself."

Boyz N the Hood opened in 1991 to almost universal critical acclaim. Reviewing the film for the *Chicago Sun Times*, Roger Ebert called the movie "one of the best American films of recent years." He went on to describe *Boyz* as "a thoughtful, realistic

Film director John Singleton (center) was honored for his significant contribution to entertainment and public service by the National Association of Black Owned Broadcasters in 1997. Here he chats with television personality Bryant Gumbel and U.S. Representative Maxine Waters, who also received awards.

look at a young man's coming of age, and also a human drama of rare power." *Washington Post* critic Rita Mawley wrote, "With its energetic cast and insistent street score, [*Boyz N the Hood*] still manages to be poignant without becoming pathetic, and violent without being exploitative." *Urban Drama Reviews* called *Boyz* "one of the best urban dramas ever made," and cited Gooding's performance as "outstanding and realistic." Movie critic Leonard Maltin called the film a "sober, thoughtful look at life in the black section of South Central L.A. . . . Impressive debut for 23-year-old writer-director Singleton."

Movie fans also responded favorably: *Boyz N the Hood* made more than $50 million at the box office.

John Singleton was just 23 when he wrote and directed *Boyz N the Hood*. It was his first movie, made on a very small budget and in the very same neighborhoods of south central Los Angeles in which Singleton had grown up. It was a great honor when he garnered an Academy Award nomination in the Best Original Screenplay category. Although the screenplay for *Boyz N the Hood* did not win the Academy Award, Singleton's movie did put him on a list of prominent African-American writer-directors that also included Spike Lee and Robert Townsend.

Boyz N the Hood also put Cuba Gooding Jr. on a noteworthy list: a publication called John Willis' *Screen World* named him one of 12 Promising New Actors of 1991. He enjoyed the experience of filming *Boyz N the Hood* and recognized the importance of the movie. In a 1992 interview with the *Chicago Tribune*, Gooding expressed concern that although journalists and award-givers would pay *Boyz* a certain amount of lip service, the film would remain rigidly categorized as a "black" movie. "This is a good time for black actors and directors and producers," he said. "But we have to continue to progress if we're going to be completely accepted. There's still an element of 'Oh, *Boyz N the Hood* was a good movie—for a black film.' There's still a weird vibe out there."

After *Boyz N the Hood*, however, Gooding's career seemed immune to any adverse "vibes." His performance in *Boyz* had put his name on the list of young black actors to be reckoned with. It seemed that Gooding—who had gone from riches to rags and who now appeared to be headed back to riches again—was guaranteed to become a star.

Or was he?

4

HARD LUCK

❧

Although Cuba's future in films seemed assured, his career stalled after Boyz N the Hood. He took supporting roles, such as that of the boxer Lincoln, shown here opposite veteran actor Brian Dennehy, in the fight film Gladiator. The film was a critical failure. It seemed that Cuba's acting career was moving backwards.

AFTER THE CRITICAL and commercial success of *Boyz N the Hood*, Cuba Gooding Jr. began work on his next movie, a boxing drama called *Gladiator*. He also appeared in a made-for-television movie called *Murder Without Motive*, based on the true story of the 1985 shooting death of a young black man at the hands of an undercover police officer in New York City.

Gooding had been less than enthusiastic about *Gladiator* when he was first offered the script. One of Gooding's distinguishing characteristics is his insistence that the roles he plays—and the movies he chooses to appear in—be endowed with positive traits and themes that transcend stereotypes.

"I look for films that teach something positive," Gooding told *Scholastic Update* magazine in 1992 before the release of *Gladiator*. In that same interview, Gooding noted that he had initially turned down his role in the film. "When I read the first *Gladiator* script I thought it was stupid. My character was going 'Yo,' 'what fo' and 'what mo.' And it was only the white kid who walks off victorious, after facing the perils of the black and Hispanic community on the south side of Chicago. Bull." It was only after substantial script revisions that Gooding eventually agreed to play the part of Lincoln in the Rowdy Herrington–directed movie. The salary was also nice: Gooding had earned $32,000 for his part in *Boyz*; he would receive $100,000 for *Gladiator*.

The plot of *Gladiator* is something of a mixture of *Boyz N the Hood* and the now-classic boxing movie *Rocky*. An honors high school student named Tommy (James Marshall) moves with his father to a tough neighborhood on Chicago's south side when his father gets into financial trouble with the mob. At first, the neighborhood kids taunt Tommy, but he soon proves to be a talented fighter. Tommy is so talented, in fact, that he attracts the attention of a rather seedy boxing promoter (Brian Dennehy), who begins booking the youngster in semipro bouts.

One of the crooked promoter's other clients is a tough-guy-with-a-heart-of-gold type named Lincoln, played by Cuba Gooding Jr. Lincoln and Tommy have both sold their souls, in a sense: the fights the promoter books for them more closely resemble gladiator bouts than boxing matches. Fighters hit one another below the belt, break each other's jaws on a regular basis, rub irritating substances into one another's eyes, and keep slugging even after their opponents lose consciousness. The promoter, meanwhile, sets the odds with the spectators, and at the end of each bout, collects a profit from the gambling. Tommy is repelled by the violence and ugliness of these fights, but the promoter gets control over Tommy's father by paying off his gambling debts, leaving Tommy trapped in the dismal world of this so-called sport until his father can pay back the promoter.

Tommy is the protagonist of the movie—the one who ultimately gets to fight the promoter in a climactic boxing scene—but Lincoln's story makes for an interesting sidebar to Tommy's. A talented boxer in his own right, Lincoln also gets caught up in the promoter's world, and like Tommy, has trouble breaking free. But Lincoln faces challenges outside of the ring as well—struggles that Gooding deemed realistic enough to make the character appealing.

"Lincoln starts out selfish, but he changes, and you see goodness coming out of him," Gooding observed in a 1992 interview with the *Chicago Tribune*. "He's a kid who's grown up in a black and Hispanic community where there's a lot of gang violence, and he has had to fight. He finds out he's good with his fists. Then he gets caught up in these illegal boxing bouts, and he's really good at them, and he's thinking he's going to go pro."

In *Gladiator*, Lincoln gets a girl pregnant and has a daughter. This changes his perspective on life, Gooding explained in the *Tribune* interview.

"Now he's thinking he doesn't want his little girl to have to face the things he has had to face. So he's really fighting for his little girl." At the end, Lincoln, like Tommy, decides to break away from the seedy promoter and the dirty fights. Tommy and Lincoln are united by this mutual goal. "And at the end, it doesn't matter that one of the boxers is black and the other is white. They both come together to fight the ultimate evil, the boxing promoter, and they both learn something about themselves," Gooding remarked.

Reviews of *Gladiator* were mixed. Desson Howe wrote in the *Washington Post*, "*Gladiator* is utter trash masquerading as an action picture with a message." But Howe did have good things to say about Marshall and Gooding, both of whom he credited with "strong, authoritative performances." The critic went on to say that "Gooding is engaging and wise-talking." Writing in the same publication, Rita Kempley stated, "Gooding has the angelic good looks of Isaiah Thomas and invests Lincoln with courageous sweetness. It's too bad the part isn't better developed."

On the whole Cuba, who had received top billing, fared better with the critics than did the movie itself. But moviegoers didn't seem to be interested

in buying a ticket for a movie that appeared to be a *Rocky* knockoff, and *Gladiator* did not do particularly well at the box office. Another film he made in 1992, *Hitz*, an action movie about the trial of a Los Angeles gang member, was not well received critically. He also took a small part in a TV movie called *Daybreak*. Released in 1993, *Daybreak* was a futuristic love story about two young resistance fighters battling a fascist regime. After finishing filming,

he agreed to play the role of a corporal in a highly anticipated movie—the Rob Reiner–directed film *A Few Good Men.*

After Gooding's star turns in *Boyz N the Hood* and *Gladiator,* his role in *A Few Good Men* was surprisingly small. Gooding's character, Corporal Carl Hammaker, appears in only a few scenes of the movie, about the trial of two Marines accused of murder on the military base at Guantanamo Bay, Cuba. But the film did allow him to work with an incredible ensemble of Hollywood talent: Tom Cruise, Jack Nicholson, Demi Moore, Kevin Bacon, Kiefer Sutherland, and Kevin Pollak.

In the film, Cruise plays a cocky young lawyer who must defend the two alleged murderers. He is assisted by Moore and Pollak, while Bacon acts as the prosecutor. Kiefer Sutherland is good as a Marine officer, and veteran actor Jack Nicholson

Cuba finally got a chance to act in a critically acclaimed, big-budget film when he appeared with Tom Cruise, Demi Moore, and Kevin Pollak (left to right) in A Few Good Men. Although his role was still small, he gained the experience of working with a talented cast. His relationship with Cruise was a stroke of luck that would eventually lead to their costarring in the blockbuster film Jerry Maguire.

turned in an Academy Award–nominated performance as the commander of the Marine base where the murders occurred. In the climactic courtroom scenes, Gooding's character provides crucial evidence for the defense. Although the presence of so many big-name stars made it less likely he would be noticed by the critics, Gooding's performance was solid and thoughtful.

A *Few Good Men* marked Cuba Gooding Jr.'s first high-profile, big-budget film. When it was released in December 1992, *A Few Good Men* went up against several other blockbusters, including *The Bodyguard*, *Dracula*, and *Aladdin*. Nevertheless, the movie did very well at the box office, earning more than $100 million. It also won some critical raves, receiving four Academy Award nominations, including Best Picture.

After completing work on *A Few Good Men*, Gooding costarred in a movie called *Judgment Night*, directed by Stephen Hopkins. *Judgment Night* is the story of four friends in Chicago. When they get lost on their way to a boxing match and end up in a bad area of the city, they witness a mob-style murder and are seen by the killers, who then pursue them relentlessly.

Hollywood veteran Emilio Estevez plays the main character; caustic comedian Dennis Leary shows his menacing side as the film's villain. Gooding portrays Mike Peterson, a young man with human frailties similar to those of Lincoln, the character he played in *Gladiator* the previous year. Although Peterson may seem like a bland, clichéd character to some viewers, Gooding enjoyed playing him. "I had a lot of fun with this character," he told *American Visions* in 1993, the year *Judgment Night* was released. Gooding acknowledged that Peterson is far from a heroic figure, but asserted that his character "provides courage and hope throughout the darkest times in the movie."

Many who saw *Judgment Night* might attest that

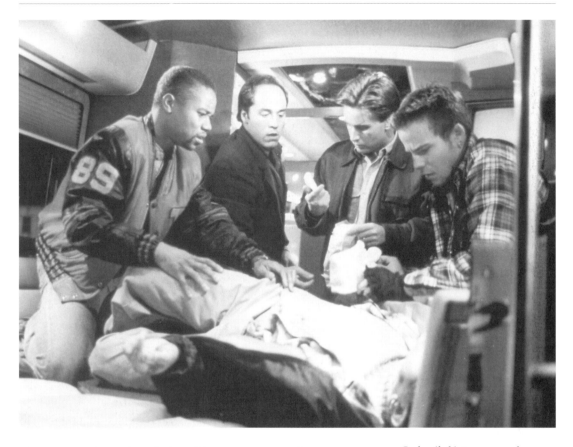

Cuba (left) in a scene from Judgment Night. *Although the film was harshly criticized, Cuba enjoyed playing the character of Mike Peterson, and he received good reviews for his performance.*

the entire length of the film constituted a pretty dark time. Critics universally panned the movie. Writing in the *Washington Post*, Richard Harrington called the film "regrettably familiar fare," and suggested that viewers craving a stronger plot might prefer *Bonfire of the Vanities* or *Grand Canyon*, two other recent releases that depicted accidental wrong turns and their consequences. Harrington went on to comment that there is "precious little tension in this cat-and-louse tale, and certainly none of the racial tension one might expect." He did save his kindest words for Gooding, however, who he described as "solid" in his role.

But even Gooding could not escape the devastating comments of online critic James Berardinelli, who said that the actor "flounders" in his portrayal of Peterson. Berardinelli, who called *Judgment Night* "one of the most unbearably dull 'thrillers' of the year," also suggested that perhaps Gooding should find a new agent. "Since *Boyz N the Hood* his parts (which include the dull but brainless *Gladiator* and the anything-but-fun *Daybreak*) have gotten less challenging and more clichéd."

Gooding (who later would indeed change agents and publicists several times) did not heed Berardinelli's advice in 1993. Instead he agreed to play the part of Ben Doyle in an action comedy called *Lightning Jack*, a starring vehicle for Australian actor Paul Hogan of *Crocodile Dundee* fame. Written and produced by Hogan, *Lightning Jack* is the story of an Australian macho man who travels through the American west after fighting in the Civil War. Jack kidnaps Ben (Gooding), who is mute. After some initial antagonism, the two team up and adopt a life of crime.

Gooding, whose pantomime talent had earned him an acting award during high school, was eager to take on the challenge of playing a man who could not speak. "I'm so excited about this role," he told *American Visions* while filming *Lightning Jack* in 1993. "It could end up being my favorite. It's on a lighter note, but it still has that quality that all of my other characters have had." He would receive $500,000—his highest paycheck to date—for making the movie.

The actor was happy to accept another essentially upbeat role, and his turn as Ben Doyle did garner some critical praise. But on the whole, critics did not care for *Lightning Jack*. In the *Chicago Sun Times*, Roger Ebert decried the plot as "a meandering story that exists primarily as a peg for Hogan's personality." Ebert went on to say that the humor in *Lightning Jack* relied much too heavily on clichéd, predictable jokes. He did, however, allow that Gooding was innovative in his portrayal of Ben Doyle, acknowledging that

Gooding "creates an entirely different kind of character, and is willing to mug and pantomime to get his
message across."

Deseret News movie critic Chris Hicks complained that *Lightning Jack* "is sluggish and too long."
But Hicks chose much kinder words when discussing
Gooding's contribution to the film, citing the actor's
formidable comic talent. "Whenever Gooding is on
the screen," Hicks wrote, "he steals the picture. A
talented dramatic actor, Gooding is hilarious here,
offering up some wonderful pantomime slapstick, yet

*Anxious to play an upbeat
character, Cuba accepted the
role of the mute Ben Doyle,
here in a scene with costar Paul
Hogan (left) in Lightning Jack.
Even though the film was
panned and was a box-office
flop, critics praised Cuba's
comic talents.*

there is also an air of dignity to his disadvantaged and disenfranchised character."

A review in *TV Guide Online* also praised Gooding but blamed the film's writers for creating under-developed characters. "Gooding gets as much mileage as he can out of Ben Doyle, but the character is so saccharine he makes *Huckleberry Finn*'s runaway slave Jim look like a firebrand," wrote the reviewer. "The relationship between Ben and Jack never really develops any warmth or resonance, mainly because it seems never to have been thought through."

Unfortunately, the positive reviews Gooding received for his work in *Lightning Jack* could not save the picture itself: fans stayed away in droves. Gooding's star was descending fast: three of his last four movies had been critical and commercial failures.

His personal life was flourishing at this time, however. Gooding had recently married Sara Kapfer, his high school sweetheart.

As for his career woes, the actor did not sit idly waiting for theatrical film roles; he added to his repertoire of projects with television work. Perhaps Gooding's most important professional endeavor during the five years between *Boyz N the Hood* and *Jerry Maguire* was *The Tuskegee Airmen*, a drama produced for the Home Box Office (HBO) cable network in 1995. *The Tuskegee Airmen* is based on the true story of an all-black platoon in the United States Army during World War II. African Americans have served in every war in this country's history, including the American Revolution. Until relatively recently, however, blacks who fought in the nation's military campaigns served in units completely segregated from the white units. Not surprisingly, these African-American units were considered less important than the white ones. Accordingly, they were paid lower wages and given second-rate equipment and clothing.

Another movie that explored the African-American war effort was the 1989 Civil War movie

The HBO production of The Tuskegee Airmen *gave Cuba a strong dramatic role when he played pilot Billy Roberts. The cast included Laurence Fishburne (in front next to Cuba), with whom he had appeared in* Boyz, *as well as Allen Payne and Malcolm-Jamal Warner.*

Glory (which featured Denzel Washington in an Oscar-winning performance). Like the black squadron in *Glory*, the African-American force in *The Tuskegee Airmen* is segregated and considered inferior to the rest of the armed forces. The African-American pilots fight to prove that the color of a man's skin has no bearing on his intelligence or on his ability to fly fighter planes. Despite the prejudice of the military brass in their own country, 445 Tuskegee airmen flew in overseas combat. From 1943 to 1945, these pilots participated in some of America's most dangerous military missions.

Against all odds, none of their planes were lost to enemy aircraft, although 66 of the Tuskegee pilots did die in battle. The black airmen received more than 850 medals for their courage under fire. Still, most Americans remained oblivious to the remarkable achievements of the Tuskegee Airmen, who returned home to racism and discrimination at the war's end. (For more information on the Tuskegee Airmen, see the appendix on page 93).

Despite a riveting plot line and strong performances by both Gooding (who played pilot Billy Roberts) and Laurence Fishburne (who had played Gooding's father in *Boyz* and portrayed a fellow pilot in this film), the movie received only lukewarm reviews. "Surprisingly lifeless," Curt Schleier of the *Detroit News* said of *The Tuskegee Airmen*, while critic Leonard Maltin rated the movie average but praised the actors, calling *Airmen* a "rather pedestrian war movie elevated somewhat by a first-rate cast." Although Gooding got to portray a positive role model of the highest order in the movie, his value in Hollywood was continuing to decline.

In 1995, Gooding was still working, but the number of movie offers—which had been plentiful four years earlier with the success of *Boyz N the Hood*—was dwindling. One offer Gooding happily accepted was from director Wolfgang Peterson, who was casting for *Outbreak*, a movie about a lethal virus. Peterson remembered Gooding's performance in *Boyz*. Gooding recalled how he landed a role in *Outbreak* in a 1997 interview with *Ebony* magazine. "Wolfgang Peterson called me in," Gooding said, "and goes, 'Cuba, you remember me from that time in the elevator at the *Boyz* premiere and I told you that you were great in the movie? And we should work together.' That's how I got the part in *Outbreak*."

Although he was pleased to join an impressive cast that included Dustin Hoffman, Rene Russo,

Kevin Spacey, Morgan Freeman, and Donald Sutherland, Cuba's salaries per film were falling along with his appeal in Hollywood: he received $100,000 less for this film than he had for *Lightning Jack*.

In *Outbreak*, Hoffman plays Colonel Sam Daniels, a scientist at an army agency who must develop a vaccine against a deadly virus (originally carried by an infected monkey) that has broken out in a small California town. The virus is spreading fast and killing its victims swiftly, so Hoffman's research and development process becomes a race

Cuba shares the screen with big-name actors Dustin Hoffman (right) and Kevin Spacey (center) in the film Outbreak. *Tapped by director Wolfgang Peterson, who had seen his work in* Boyz, *Cuba was happy to join such Hollywood talent. His reviews were good, but he still was not being offered any major roles.*

against time. Gooding plays Major Salt, a young army scientist—and a helicopter pilot—who assists Daniels in his search for a vaccine. His is not the largest part in the film, but it is an important one.

In one scene, Salt accompanies Daniels to a location in Africa where the virus has already killed a number of people. The colonel asks Salt if he's prepared for the gruesome sight of the virus's victims. Salt, fresh out of medical school, replies that he is prepared—he's read about all the different symptoms. "Reading about it and seeing it are two different things," Daniels responds. Salt soon discovers that his mentor is correct.

In addition to the suspenseful search for a vaccine, *Outbreak* also features a villain (Donald Sutherland) who does his best to obstruct Daniels's and Salt's progress, and a love interest for Daniels— his ex-wife (Rene Russo)—who just happens to be a scientist at the Centers for Disease Control. The combination of science, suspense, and romance makes *Outbreak* entertaining viewing. The film did score some commercial success, although it got mixed reviews.

Writing for the online movie review site *99 Lives*, Lorna Lyons and Juliette Colin praised the movie for being entertaining and suspenseful. They made special mention of the way Gooding and Hoffman interact onscreen. "The repartee between Hoffman and Gooding Jr. . . . is natural and enjoyable; they have great chemistry together," they wrote. In the *San Francisco Chronicle*, Mick LaSalle called the film "a superb thriller."

But Richard Corliss, in his review of *Outbreak* for *Time* magazine, derided the movie as a "big, bustling, intermittently dippy melodrama." *New Republic* critic Stanley Kauffmann dismissed the movie as "hyperventilated drama." The *San Francisco Examiner*'s critic, Barbara Shulgasser, didn't care for the movie either, calling it "an outbreak of boring dialogue." And critic Leonard Maltin opined, "[This] dynamite suspense thriller with a surprising sense of humor goes almost completely awry in the second half, turning Hoffman into a kind of super-hero and everyone else into a caricature or stick figure. What a shame!"

Mixed reviews aside, Gooding had shared the screen with a slew of big-name actors in *Outbreak*. Even so, he was not an automatic choice for leading roles, so he found himself auditioning for roles once again—something he probably hoped was over and done with after the success of *Boyz N the Hood*. But Gooding was still getting parts in movies: his audi-tion for *Losing Isaiah* was one such success. Gooding was cast in the role of Eddie Hughes, the fiancé of Halle Berry's character, Kailua.

The plot of *Losing Isaiah* is emotionally charged. Isaiah is an African-American child born addicted to crack because his mother, Kailua, was a drug addict who used crack while she was pregnant with him. Kailua abandons her baby when he is only a few days old, leaving him in a cardboard box in an alley one night. The next morning she regrets her action and runs to find Isaiah, but he has disap-peared. Kailua believes he has died.

But Isaiah has actually been found and taken to a hospital. He is eventually adopted by a loving white couple (Jessica Lange and David Strathairn).

A few years later, Kailua has successfully completed a drug rehabilitation program and is beginning to put her life back together. She meets and becomes engaged to a charming and decent man named Eddie (Gooding). Around this time, she discovers quite by accident that her preschool-aged son is very much alive, and she decides to seek custody of him.

The movie presents both sides of the issue in a fair and balanced way, but *Losing Isaiah* did not strike a chord with audiences at the box office. Critics found *Losing Isaiah* to be well intentioned, but they also

Cuba and his wife, Sara Kapfer, enjoy his Oscar win at the Academy Awards. Dating since high school, the couple was married in 1994, the year in which Cuba costarred in Lightning Jack.

faulted the film for not taking a firm stand on the issues it raised. Rita Kempley of the *Washington Post* called the movie an "evenhanded melodrama [that] is neutral to a fault." Roger Ebert of the *Chicago Sun Times* complained, "The filmmakers apparently have no firm ideas of their own about the rightness and wrongness of the alternatives." But Gooding won praise for his portrayal of the appealing, supportive Eddie, although Juliette Colin of *99 Lives* complained that the talented actor could have been put to better use. Gooding, she wrote, "is a welcome presence here, but he's too good an actor to be stuck playing a stereotype."

After bursting onto the scene in the early 1990s as an African-American star on the rise, Cuba was now fighting to keep his career moving forward. After *Losing Isaiah*, Gooding was offered only a few movie parts, none of them appealing or challenging. He was stuck in a no-man's-land, waiting for his luck to change. There was no question that Cuba Gooding Jr. needed a hit to resurrect his flagging career.

5

"SHOW ME THE MONEY!"

❦

Cuba finally got a chance to see the money when, after years in a slump, he got the role of football player Rod Tidwell in Jerry Maguire, *the role that propelled him into the top ranks of film actors. Cuba has credited the generous support of costar Tom Cruise (here with Cuba on the set) with helping him to give such a powerful performance.*

BY 1995, CUBA Gooding Jr. had to face a sad but inevitable truth: his star, which had burned so brightly after his electrifying performance in *Boyz N the Hood*, was fading quickly. In fact, it had all but burned out.

Mired in a serious career slump, Gooding was told that he couldn't expect to receive offers for good starring roles or top-dollar payment for the movie parts he did get. His predicament was a very difficult pill to swallow. Just a few years after scoring such critical raves in *Boyz*, he was now a second-tier actor. Barely in his mid-twenties, Gooding found himself being treated like a has-been.

But Gooding kept working even though his appeal had dropped. He was able to look at his past failures realistically, and he refused to give up. He remained confident that eventually he would regain the prominence that had virtually fallen into his lap such a short time ago. "I told myself, 'Look bro, the *Boyz N the Hood* days are gone,'" he later told the *New York Times*. "You've got to do what you've got to do to get back up there."

Gooding was too gifted an actor to be continually playing small roles, but he continued to work in order to ensure that his name would not disappear completely from the roster of talented young black actors competing for a small amount of plum roles.

Cameron Crowe, who wrote the screenplay for Jerry Maguire, *was so impressed by Cuba's auditions and his determination to play Rod Tidwell that he rewrote Cuba's character to fit the young actor's physical size.*

He was jockeying for roles against the likes of Denzel Washington, Wesley Snipes, and Will Smith. Gooding could not afford to simply disappear while he waited for a high-profile project to find him.

Fortunately, during the filming of *Outbreak*, Gooding's agent called to tell him that Cameron

Crowe, a young writer and director, had written a screenplay called *Jerry Maguire*. It was about a sports agent and his only client, an arrogant football player. Damon Wayans, Crowe's first choice for the role, was not available to make the movie, so Gooding's agent wondered if he wanted to read for the part of the football player. Both agent and actor knew it was a long shot, but Gooding agreed to audition for the role, figuring he had nothing to lose.

He also knew that it was up to him to present himself as memorably as possible. But Gooding didn't have much time to prepare—the audition was scheduled for the very same day that he learned about the part. He hadn't even seen the script!

Fortunately, he did manage to get a copy before the audition, and he quickly read through the script. By the time he arrived on the studio lot for his audition, Gooding knew that he definitely wanted to play the cocky football player, Rod Tidwell.

Gooding naturally expected to read Tidwell's lines opposite Tom Cruise, who had already been cast in the title role. But when he arrived at the audition, he learned that Cruise had been unable to make it, and that Robin Williams would be standing in for him. Although he had never met Williams, Gooding quickly felt a comfortable rapport with him. They batted the lines back and forth with rapid energy. The movie's producer, James Brooks, was taken by what he saw. "We were wildly impressed," he told the *New York Times*. Crowe, who was also present at Gooding's audition, was similarly bowled over by the actor's performance. "From that moment on," he told the *Times*, "we thought of Cuba as our man of destiny." Crowe saw Gooding to the door and told him that he was most definitely a contender for the role.

Although Gooding had dazzled both the director and the producer of *Jerry Maguire*, one major

Even in playing a scene alone, shouting into the telephone, Cuba's talent at carrying a scene, and sometimes stealing it, was apparent. He admitted that, in order to get the role, he verbally abused Tom Cruise during the auditions.

concern lingered about casting him as a football player: his size. Even though he had a trim, athletic build, at five feet eleven inches tall Gooding didn't really have the stature or bulk to be a realistic choice to portray a bruising, powerful pro football player. Aware that his size might prevent him from getting the role, Gooding decided to do what he could to resemble the athlete he so desperately wanted to play. He immediately embarked on a strict workout regimen, lifting weights every day.

Cuba had also shown up at the first audition with a shaved head and tried to convince the director and producer that this was in character for a driven, over-the-top football player like Rod Tidwell. In fact, he had shaved his head for another audition, and his hair had not yet grown back. "I originally did it for an audition for *The Fan*, which I didn't get," he later admitted. "Lost to John Leguizamo. So I said, 'I see this character [Tidwell] bald'—because I was bald already."

Gooding kept his shaved head for the second audition, and he wore a T-shirt that was too small to show off his more muscular physique. This time, he did read opposite Tom Cruise. Again, all who were present—Cruise included—were impressed by Gooding's performance. Crowe and Brooks told Gooding they'd call him and that he was still very much in the running, but they made no promises. They were still worried that Gooding simply was not big enough to make a convincing football player.

But Crowe eventually adjusted his vision of Rod Tidwell slightly to make Gooding a viable choice for the role. He rewrote the character of Tidwell as a wide receiver—a position where his lack of bulk would not seem unrealistic—and also added several references to his lack of height to the script. Gooding was called back for a third audition. This time, the actor went for broke. Realizing that Rod Tidwell was a character who could steal every scene he was in, Gooding played off Cruise aggressively. "I really didn't know what they wanted from me anymore," the actor later recalled, "so I just went in there and banged Tom around the room with lines, verbally abusing him." At last, Crowe and company ended the waiting game and offered Gooding the part.

Gooding had just landed the role of his career. *Jerry Maguire* would turn out to be one of the best sports movies ever made. The film not only focuses on the high and low points of professional sports but also interweaves the developing relationships between the characters in an appealing and believable way.

The movie opens with a voice-over by Cruise, who plays Jerry Maguire, explaining in a rather cocky manner just how busy and successful he is as a top agent at Sport Marketing International (SMI). Maguire has 72 clients, many of them top-drawer athletes looking for an agent who knows the score to protect their interests.

The film shows scenes of Maguire dealing with his athlete clients. These images are not idealized and uplifting, but depressing and almost shameful. In one scene, Cruise is at the hospital bedside of an injured hockey player. The player has clearly suffered a concussion: he's having trouble remembering the names of his wife and son. It is also evident that this is not the player's first serious injury. Even so, he is anxious to get back on the ice for his next game. "I get that bonus if I play in 90 percent of all my games," he explains to his horrified wife.

The player's son catches up with Maguire in the hospital hallway and asks him to please give his father a break because he needs to recover. Maguire tells the boy that it's going to take a lot more than an injury to keep his father off the ice. The player's son shakes his head, swears at Maguire, and walks away. For Maguire, the boy's outrage serves as a wake-up call. "There was only one thing wrong," his voice-over monologue continues, "I hated myself. Or rather, I hated my place in the world."

Not long after his confrontation with the hockey player's son, Maguire suffers a panic attack in the middle of the night. In a fit of desperate eloquence, he sits down at his computer and produces a moving and emotional 25-page mission statement. Entitled *The Things We Think and Do Not Say*, the work conveys Maguire's dismay that he and his fellow agents have let their greed for money and prestige get in the way of what is most important. In sum, the statement stresses that the company should concentrate more on taking care of its clients, rather than on making as much money as possible. "Fewer clients, less money," he writes.

Maguire stuffs his mission statement into every mailbox at SMI. Although he gets a standing ovation when he arrives at the office after distributing the statement, he is unceremoniously fired one week later at a business lunch. Back at the office, Maguire desperately tries to keep his athlete clients from abandoning him. He makes phone call after phone call, only to find that most of his clients have either transferred their loyalty to other agents at SMI, or are speaking to Bob Sugar, the agent who has just dismissed Jerry, and are in the process of dropping Maguire as their representative. At the end of the day, all of Jerry Maguire's clients have abandoned him—save for one short, scrappy, second-rate wide receiver by the name of Rod Tidwell.

Tidwell's uninspired performance on the field does not reflect his true talent. Maguire has therefore long viewed Tidwell as a lackluster client who will never really rake in big bucks for himself—or for anyone representing him. But Maguire phones him anyway, asking him to stay on as a client. Rather than accepting Maguire's offer on the spot, Tidwell makes his agent work for the privilege of keeping him. "Here's what I want you to do for me, Jerry," Tidwell cajoles. "It's very simple. It's like a mantra in my family. Are you ready? Here it is: 'Show me the money.' Now I want to hear you say it."

Maguire, eager to nab Tidwell and call other clients, barely complies. "Show you the money," he says lamely.

"No, no man, I want you to really say it," says Tidwell. " 'Show me the money.' Like it's happening to you."

Cuba prepared for his role as an underachieving but still cocky football player by studying the talk and behavior—and attitudes—of professional players.

"Show me the money."

"Okay, now really say it. Like, shout it, man. 'Show me the money!'"

"Show me the money."

"Louder, Jerry, come on. Bob Sugar's on the other line, man. Come on. 'SHOW ME THE MONEY! SHOW ME THE MONEY!'"

In complete desperation, Maguire complies:

"SHOW ME THE MONEY!! SHOW ME THE MONEY!!" he shouts.

After making Maguire jump through a few more hoops, Tidwell ends their conversation. "Congratulations, Jerry. You're still my agent."

A volatile bond soon develops between Maguire and Tidwell. The basis of their relationship is, of course, business. Tidwell, playing out the option year of his contract, wants Maguire to negotiate a four-year, $10 million extension for him. Tidwell's team makes a paltry offer of a one-year, $1 million contract. Tidwell, with his wife's encouragement, rejects the offer and elects to become a free agent.

A friendship forms between the two men, despite their strongly voiced opinions on one another's weaknesses. Maguire initially views Tidwell with a combination of gratitude and annoyance. He is grateful that Tidwell has remained loyal to him, but he is also annoyed by the athlete's constant complaints about being forever underappreciated, underexposed, and underpaid. Tidwell, for his part, is resentful because Maguire never paid proper attention to him previously, when he was too busy reaping glory and money from his more illustrious then-clients.

At the end of one game—in which Tidwell performed decently but didn't make any big plays—he starts complaining to Maguire yet again about how he's less appreciated than his teammates, oblivious to the fact that he's not as successful on the field as they are.

"Okay, so we're friends, so I can tell you why it is that you're not getting paid what you should be getting paid," Maguire tells Tidwell. "It's because you're playing with this (Maguire points to his head) instead of this (pointing to his heart). All you care about is what you get from this game, not what you're giving, or how much you love football." Tidwell is initially steamed at Maguire's assessment.

"I don't want to be friends anymore," he says. But he also knows that his agent is right: he has to find his passion for the game.

In true Hollywood fashion, Tidwell goes on to have a storybook season that leads to a climactic scene in which Tidwell, who has landed on his head after catching the ball in the end zone for a touchdown, lies motionless. Maguire runs onto the field, now more concerned about his friend's well-being than with the profit potential of his client. Several long minutes pass. Then Tidwell regains consciousness, jumps to his feet, and performs perhaps the greatest post-touchdown celebration ever executed on the gridiron. Gooding's Tidwell actually break dances a little, performing moves reminiscent of the actor's first professional performance, which had taken place at the Olympic closing ceremonies over a decade earlier.

Gooding had clearly done his homework for the role of Rod Tidwell. After getting the part, he spent a great deal of time with professional football players, learning how they behaved, how they spoke, and how they displayed a confident attitude on the field. Gooding's preparation shows in his performance. With his cocky, confident—and at times sulky—manner, Gooding steals virtually every scene he appears in.

The relationship between *Jerry Maguire*'s star and supporting actor was part of what made Gooding's powerful performance possible. Gooding and Tom Cruise had met four years earlier when Gooding played a small role in *A Few Good Men*, in which Cruise starred. But the two had not spent much time together then. In fact, when *Jerry Maguire* started shooting, Gooding figured that the star would be rather standoffish. After all, Tom Cruise was one of the biggest names in Hollywood, making $20 million per picture, while Cuba Gooding was earning just $600,000. But Cruise turned out to be a generous colleague. "I've worked with actors like that, big, big name actors, and sometimes you get into a situation where they allow you to do just enough to enhance their performance, and that's it," Gooding said in praise of Cruise in the *Toronto Star*. "And yet he was always allowing me to give for him, and then he'd give back for me. He'd say, 'Don't forget [Gooding's] close up.' That's the first time I'd heard a fellow actor say that. It was really an amazing movie experience for me."

The bond apparently endured long after production had wrapped up on *Jerry Maguire*. After both Cruise and Gooding garnered Oscar nominations for their work in the movie (Cameron Crowe was also nominated for Best Original Screenplay), they celebrated one another's good news over the telephone. Gooding told *USA Today*, "We screamed at each other for ten minutes. It was nothing intelligent, just 'Arrrggghhh. Ahhh. Yeaaahhh!' I yelled. He yelled. Then he went hoarse."

Gooding's acting had been amazing, and it won him tremendous critical raves. Writing for the online movie review site *99 Lives*, Scott Renshaw called Gooding's performance an "electrifying delight," and Leonard Maltin described Cuba as "charismatic." In her review of the movie for the *Washington Post*, Rita Kempley enthused that Gooding "just about walks off with the movie with his ebullient grandstanding."

Gooding was honored for his role in *Jerry Maguire* with a Golden Globe Award for best performance by a supporting actor in a movie musical or comedy, and of course, he also won the coveted Academy Award in the spring of 1997. But perhaps more importantly, the movie had given Cuba Gooding Jr. the opportunity not only to get his career back on track but also to make a statement of his own about the most important things in life. "Because Rod wants Jerry Maguire to show him the

An ebullient Cuba hugs costar Tom Cruise after winning the Oscar. The two actors formed a friendship while making Jerry Maguire, *and their relationship continued long after the film was released.*

money," Gooding told the *New York Times*, "some people think the movie is about money, but it's not. It's about respect."

With his performance in *Jerry Maguire*, Gooding had earned the respect of his peers in the movie industry. He was back in the limelight. Now he had to find a way to stay there.

6

LIFE AFTER OSCAR

❧

WITH AN OSCAR on his shelf and a smash movie on his resumé, Cuba Gooding Jr. was once again a big name in Hollywood, with scripts and movie offers coming to him daily. He had hardly been waiting around for his big break, however. His participation in a small, little-known film called *Do Me a Favor* is evidence of this. The 1996 movie, which tells the story of the criminal escapades of an alluring woman with a menacing boyfriend, is frequently omitted from filmographies of Gooding's work. But the actor's next big-budget movie appearance after *Jerry Maguire* was actually already filmed even before he won his Academy Award. In fact, Gooding had been making *Jerry Maguire* when he was cast as Frank Sachs in the James Brooks comedy *As Good As It Gets*.

An offbeat romantic comedy, *As Good As It Gets* stars Jack Nicholson as a completely unpleasant novelist who suffers from obsessive-compulsive disorder. Nicholson's character, Melvin Udall, manages to offend anyone and everyone he meets, from a waitress at a neighborhood restaurant named Carol (Helen Hunt) to his homosexual neighbor, Simon (Greg Kinnear). Simon, who is an artist, has a tough but kind-hearted agent named Frank Sachs, portrayed by Cuba Gooding Jr.

When Simon needs Melvin Udall's help, Sachs

After his Oscar win, Cuba won a starring role with Robin Williams in What Dreams May Come. *He and Williams and costar Annabella Sciorra celebrate the announcement of the then forthcoming film, in which Cuba plays Albert, an angel who guides Williams through the afterlife following his untimely death in a car crash.*

75

physically threatens the self-centered author and makes him promise to assist Simon.

Listed fourth in the acting credits for *As Good As It Gets*, Gooding is on target as the tough-talking art agent. Playing Frank Sachs, a cultured, bisexual art lover, was a bit of a switch from portraying the very macho Rod Tidwell in *Jerry Maguire*. But Gooding enjoyed the challenge. With Jack Nicholson's encouragement, he also made the most of his opportunity to shove one of America's most celebrated film actors against a wall during the scene in which Frank Sachs coerces Melvin Udall into helping Simon. In the scene, Gooding appears commanding and confident. In truth, however, he was initially apprehensive about roughing up Nicholson.

"I was terrified the day I had to slam Jack Nicholson into a wall," Gooding admitted in a *Calgary Sun* interview. "I asked him if there was a particular way he wanted me to grab him and to cushion the blow. He told me just to do it and not worry about him. He told me it was my scene, not his. I wore four-inch heels that day so I'd look more menacing."

One detail that might have enhanced his menacing image was Gooding's bald head, already clean-shaven for his role in *Jerry Maguire*. His hairstyle—or lack thereof—was less a choice than a necessity. He was still shooting retakes for *Jerry Maguire* when filming for *As Good As It Gets* began, so he continued to shave his head to maintain continuity.

Gooding, always extremely generous in praise of his costars, had nothing but kind words for Nicholson. " I expected Jack to be really reclusive. He's not at all. He's only distant because of other people's preconceptions of him," he told the *Calgary Sun*. "We're nervous so he backs off until we feel comfortable around him. He really taught me the love of the business. He told me if I really loved acting and put my heart into it, I could be around for

In As Good As It Gets, Cuba's character, Frank Sachs, was a bisexual art lover and Jack Nicholson's nemesis. The role was a departure from Cuba's previous roles, but he enjoyed the challenge and scored high marks from the critics.

as long as he has and still enjoy being on a set as if it were my first movie."

In that same interview, Gooding spoke about playing Frank Sachs, a character who met Gooding's moral character requirements. The fact that Sachs was bisexual was, to Gooding, a nonissue. "Sexuality is a frame of mind. The only actor who would be nervous about playing a gay character would be someone who's not secure about his own sexuality."

As Good As It Gets scored high marks with both

moviegoers and critics. The film grossed more than $30 million, and it pleased most reviewers. Janet Maslin of the *New York Times* called the film "as winning as it is barbed." Writing for the *Los Angeles Times*, Kenneth Turan praised Gooding for "reaffirming the positive impression he made in *Jerry Maguire*."

The film also made an impression at the Academy Awards in 1998. Vying for top picture honors against the blockbuster movie *Titanic, As Good As It Gets* did not take home the best motion picture Oscar, but it did boast the winners of both the Best Actor and Best Actress awards (Jack Nicholson and Helen Hunt). Greg Kinnear earned a nomination for Best Actor in a Supporting Role, although he did not win. Gooding may not have been nominated for his performance in the film, but it is worth noting that *As Good As It Gets* was the third movie in which he appeared that was nominated for the Best Motion Picture category. *A Few Good Men* and *Jerry Maguire* were the other two. (Although *Boyz N the Hood* did not receive a nomination for the best movie of 1991, John Singleton had been nominated for Best Director and Best Original Screenplay.)

Gooding continued to appear on-screen in 1998. He was part of a large ensemble cast of stars in *Welcome to Hollywood*, about an unknown actor's rise to stardom. But his next big feature film, *What Dreams May Come*, put Gooding in a starring role opposite Robin Williams. The two actors had never done a movie together, but Williams had done Gooding a great service by filling in for Tom Cruise during Gooding's initial audition for the role of Rod Tidwell. Gooding and Williams had quickly established a rapport. But if viewers were expecting a laugh-a-minute interplay between these two comedic talents in *What Dreams May Come*, they were sure to be disappointed. *Dreams* is actually a very serious movie (some lighthearted moments aside) about one man's experience of life after death. Williams plays Chris, a doctor who leaves behind a widow (Anabella Sciorra) when he dies in a freak accident— just four years after the death of the couple's children in a car crash. Gooding's character is Albert, Chris's supernatural guide to the afterlife. Albert, who has secrets of his own, leads Chris through the next world, dressed in a glowing golden outfit. Gooding's character gets to do some awe-inspiring (albeit special effects–aided) tricks, like flying and walking on water. "After the special effects guys made it possible for me to walk on water, I begged them to give me a sea for me to part," Gooding jokingly told the *Calgary Sun*.

Understandably, Gooding and Williams spent time between takes discussing their own thoughts on the possibility of an afterlife. "Considering I was having these discussions with Robin, they were pretty serious," Gooding told Laura Hobson of the *Calgary Sun*. Gooding divulged his own beliefs in the same interview. "I believe in heaven and hell. I see heaven as a place where we will have our own special reality. Mine will probably be a casino because so much of my life has been a gamble."

Gooding was pleased to be playing a positive role once again. Even after his Oscar victory, he stayed true to his basic philosophy of avoiding roles that violated his personal integrity. During the filming of *What Dreams May Come*, he turned down several roles in action pictures for that very reason. One of those was the part of a young man who attempts to save his friend in the prison drama *Return to Paradise*. Although he was initially interested in the part, Gooding eventually declined it. "It was the role of a guy who is all gung ho to save his buddy, but then at the last minute abandons his principles," he explained to the *Calgary Sun*. "I liked the concept of the film, but I just couldn't sympathize with the character's decision.

"David Conrad did a great job of the role," Gooding added of the actor who ended up playing the part, "but I still don't like the character for what he does, so I'm glad I passed on it." Gooding told the *Sun* that he had also turned down other parts in action movies. "I want to take really good acting roles as opposed to event movies," he remarked.

Reviews of *What Dreams May Come* were mixed. James Berardinelli, reviewing the film for the online movie guide *99 Lives*, called the movie "affecting drama," and described Gooding's performance as "effective in a supporting role." But Stephen Holden of the *New York Times* criticized the movie for its "fatal lack of texture and psychological nuance" and carped that Gooding was "glaringly miscast" as Albert the angel, while *Entertainment Weekly* called the film an exercise in "morose sentimentality."

Gooding continues to work regularly, but not always in feature films. Television viewers may recognize him from a series of soft-drink commercials in which he plays manically energetic characters, playfully spoofing his own supercharged Oscar acceptance speech.

In the 1999 film *Instinct*, Gooding stars opposite fellow Academy Award winner Anthony Hopkins. In the movie, based on a novel by Daniel Quinn and directed by Jon Turteltaub, Hopkins plays a primatologist named Ethan Powell. After living with a group of mountain gorillas in Rwanda, Powell has savagely maimed and killed several people and gone to jail as a result. It is up to an ambitious psychiatrist named Theo Caulder (Gooding) to unlock the secrets of Powell's mind before he is judged insane and locked up forever. The fact that Powell has stopped speaking complicates Caulder's task.

According to published reports, Gooding agreed to play the driven psychiatrist for $2.5 million. This sum may sound impressive, but for an Academy Award–winning actor, it is actually somewhat low.

Appearing in a series of television commercials, Cuba has promoted soft drinks, like Pepsi ONE, with a comic, offbeat style.

However, it was Cuba's biggest paycheck to date, and he eagerly accepted the role, commenting to columnist Marilyn Beck, "If the movie is as good as I think it is, it was probably the best move of my career."

Unfortunately, Gooding's hunch turned out to be incorrect. *Instinct* was in and out of theaters faster than a charging mountain gorilla. If the review by one movie buff on the online movie site *Mr. Showbiz* is any indication, then *Instinct* was a terrible waste of the talents of its two stars: "[Director] Jon Turteltaub has now all but totaled the reputations of Anthony Hopkins and Cuba Gooding Jr. with one of the hands-down worst movies of the season, *Instinct*."

The summer of 1999 also saw Gooding attempt to inject some humor into the action comedy *Chill Factor*. Gooding plays Arlo, a fast-talking guy who finds his ice cream truck hijacked by Mason (Skeet Ulrich), who has been entrusted with a deadly chemical formula that will kill everything in its vicinity if its temperature rises above 50 degrees. The ensuing buddy-movie hilarity and misadventure failed to attract much of an audience. *TV Guide Online* reviewer Maitland McDonagh was dismissive of *Chill Factor*, writing, "None of this is especially funny, nor is it particularly exhilarating; at best it's throwaway entertainment." McDonagh also argued that Gooding was not well suited to playing a ranting, raving motormouth like Arlo.

As if Gooding had not appeared in enough films during 1999, he also starred in *A Murder of Crows*, which premiered at the Cannes film festival in the spring and was released on video in July. In this thriller, Gooding stars as disbarred lawyer Lawson Russell, an egomaniac who takes credit for writing a best-selling book after its real author is murdered. However, Russell doesn't realize that the manuscript he has stolen is actually a factual account of a series of murders. When he is hunted by FBI agents who believe that he is the author of the work, the lawyer must go on the run to find evidence that will clear his name.

A Murder of Crows was a reunion of sorts for Cuba and director Rowdy Herrington, who had directed the actor seven years earlier in *Gladiator*. It was also the first film produced by GoodBro, a production company that Gooding founded with longtime friend Derek Broes.

Cuba Gooding Jr. expects to remain busy well into the new millennium. After *A Murder of Crows* was finished, he was slated to play a genie in *The Gelfin*, an Imagine Entertainment and Universal Pictures project. His name was also linked to a film

project titled *Memphis*, in which he would play the Rev. Martin Luther King Jr.

Two other GoodBro projects that were being discussed at the end of 1999 included a film about an older black hockey player who fights to earn a spot with an NHL team and helps win a Stanley Cup, tentatively titled *Open Ice*, as well as a movie about an integrated military brigade building a strategic roadway during World War II.

Cuba made a disastrous decision when he agreed to appear in Instinct *with veteran actor and fellow Oscar winner Anthony Hopkins. Both actors' reputations suffered mightily when the film was panned as "one of the hands-down worst movies of the season."*

Chill Factor, *which was supposed to be a comedy of misadventure, emerged as a weak, unexciting film with a silly plot. Critics and audiences alike dismissed the film, and critics complained that Cuba, here with costar Skeet Ulrich, was totally miscast.*

Although it appears that he is awaiting his next hit, it is important to remember that Cuba Gooding Jr. is only in his early thirties. Twice already he has catapulted to the top of his profession: first as a young street kid with an eye to the future in *Boyz N the Hood*, then as the high-strutting and ultimately high-minded football player in *Jerry Maguire*.

In between those films, he survived a professional slump and emerged with a revitalized career. Early on, he established a personal standard governing what he would and would not do on screen. As a very young man in his early twenties—and in the midst of the heady rush of his new celebrity after *Boyz N the Hood*—he stuck to his principles, demanding revisions of his *Gladiator* role until he deemed the character to be someone worth portraying. After surviving a decline in his career that he arguably could have avoided had he chosen to put commercial success before his insistence on playing only roles he found uplifting or instructive, he remains as selective as ever when it comes to the projects he accepts.

Gooding tries to be similarly cautious with regard to his family, whom he protects from the glare of publicity. He is proud of his younger brother, Omar, who followed Cuba into an acting career and has appeared in such television series as *Hangin' With Mr. Cooper* (1992) and *Smart Guy* (1997), and films such as *Ghost Dad* (1990) and *The Ernest Green Story* (television movie, 1993). Their father, Cuba Sr., reconciled with their mother, Shirley, in 1993, but Cuba Jr. says little about his parents, other than expressing his love for them whenever he is asked to make a comment. Nor does the actor share intimate details of his life with his wife, Sara, and their two children, Spencer and Mason. Gooding acknowledges that when he and Sara, who is white, appear in public, they receive some stares, but he says that race is not an issue between them. "I never made a conscious decision to marry a white woman," he told the *Calgary Sun* in 1998. "I dated my share of African-American women, but Sara is the woman I loved. Color was never an issue."

But spending time with his young family clearly is an issue on Gooding's mind. "My wife and I made a pact," he said in an interview with the *New York Daily News*. "I'll never go two or three weeks without seeing her and the kids. That's it."

It is evident that Gooding's personal choices, like those concerning his career decisions, are based on his need to remain true to himself.

There is no question that when Cuba Gooding Jr. triumphantly strode up to the stage at the 1996 Academy Awards, he had scored a tremendous victory, not only for himself but also for all African

Cuba is proud of his younger brother Omar (left), who has also pursued an acting career. Omar has starred in several television series including Smart Guy, *in which he appeared with young Tahj Mowry.*

Americans in Hollywood. Although Gooding was the sixth African American to win an Academy Award for acting, there have been no other black acting nominees since his victory. Gooding's name now carries the clout of an Oscar winner, but he has still had trouble securing roles worthy of his talent—despite his efforts to be discriminating about the parts he accepts. With only a limited number of top-quality roles written specifically for African Americans, Gooding and other gifted black actors are at a disadvantage in Hollywood. With such stiff competition for leading roles as Denzel Washington, Wesley Snipes, and Will Smith, Gooding is hardly guaranteed a steady supply of worthwhile, specifically African-American roles that meet his personal character standards.

Cuba and his wife, Sara, who is seen here pregnant with one of the couple's two sons. An intensely private man, Cuba seldom reveals details of his personal life and dismisses prying questions about his marriage to a white woman.

On a more optimistic note, however, Hollywood movies have become much more multicultural in their casting than they once were. Denzel Washington, for example, played the part of Lorenzo in Kenneth Branaugh's 1993 movie adaptation of Shakespeare's

Whether on film or before millions of television viewers, Cuba makes the most of his comic talents and sometimes manic sense of humor. Complaining that he and late-night talk-show host Jay Leno had on the same suit, Cuba whips off his pants and whacks at Leno during a chat on The Tonight Show.

Much Ado About Nothing. In addition, many roles, such as that of Frank Sachs, the part Gooding played in *As Good As It Gets,* are not racially specific, so there is no real obstacle to African-American actors (or actors of any other ethnic group) playing them.

Even so, the fact that an actor of Gooding's caliber is not appearing in more top-quality films does signify that the movie business has a way to go before it is truly a multicultural, equal-opportunity industry. It may well be that Gooding, one of the youngest and most talented of the crop of African-American actors currently working in Hollywood, will live to reap the benefits of a truly color-blind movie community. If he does, he can only add to his impressive list of achievements.

Backstage after winning an Academy Award and giving an energetic and inspired acceptance perfor-
mance, an overjoyed Cuba points to his Oscar while posing for photographers.

CHRONOLOGY

———— ❧ ————

1968	Born January 2 to Cuba Sr. and Shirley Gooding in New York City
1972	The Main Ingredient, Cuba Gooding Sr.'s musical group, records the smash hit "Everybody Plays the Fool"; the Gooding family moves to Southern California
1984	Performs break-dancing routine during the closing ceremonies at the 1984 Olympic Games
1986	Meets and begins dating Sara Kapfer; graduates from high school; appears on the television comedy *Amen*
1988	Receives first film role, in the Eddie Murphy film *Coming to America*
1989	Makes the movie *Sing*, which fails at the box office
1991	*Boyz N the Hood* released; the movie is praised by critics and earns more than $50 million; Gooding is named one of 12 Promising New Actors of 1991 by *Screen World*
1992	Appears in the television movie *Murder Without Motive*; gets top billing for *Gladiator*, a boxing film that flops at the box office; takes a small role in *A Few Good Men*
1993	*Judgment Night*, also starring Emilio Estevez and Dennis Leary, is released
1994	Marries Sara Kapfer; costars in *Lightning Jack* with Paul Hogan
1995	Costars in *The Tuskegee Airmen*, an HBO movie; appears in *Outbreak*; wins part of Rod Tidwell in the film *Jerry Maguire*; receives praise for his minor role in *Losing Isaiah*
1996	*Jerry Maguire* is released; Gooding receives a Golden Globe Award, and is nominated for an Academy Award; appears in the film *Do Me a Favor*; films the movie *As Good As It Gets*
1997	Receives Academy Award as Best Supporting Actor for role in *Jerry Maguire* on March 24; *As Good As It Gets* is released to critical acclaim
1998	Costars with Robin Williams in *What Dreams May Come*
1999	Has starring role in the film *Instinct*; appears in *Chill Factor* and *A Murder of Crows*

FILMOGRAPHY

—— ❧ ——

MOVIES

Coming to America (1988)
Sing (1989)
Boyz N the Hood (1991)
Gladiator (1992)
Hitz (1992)
A Few Good Men (1992)
Judgment Night (1993)
Lightning Jack (1994)
Outbreak (1995)
Losing Isaiah (1995)
Do Me a Favor (1996)
Jerry Maguire (1996)
As Good As It Gets (1997)
Welcome to Hollywood (1998)
What Dreams May Come (1998)
Chill Factor (1999)
Instinct (1999)
A Murder of Crows (1999)

TELEVISION APPEARANCES

Amen (series) (1986)
No Means No (movie) (1988)
MacGyver (series) (1989–1991)
Murder Without Motive: The Edmund Perry Story (movie) (1992)
Cool People/Hot Places (movie) (1993)
Daybreak (movie) (1993)
Kill or Be Killed (movie) (1993)
The Tuskegee Airmen (movie) (1995)

COMMERCIALS

Burger King, Bugle Boy Jeans, Sprite, Pepsi ONE

THE TUSKEGEE AIRMEN

The Tuskegee Airmen were a group of young African Americans who were taught how to operate aircraft at Alabama's Tuskegee Army Air Field during and immediately following the Second World War. At that time the American armed forces were segregated; Tuskegee represented the only training center for black aviators serving in the U.S. Army Air Force. (It was not until after the war that the air force became a branch of the military separate from the army.)

Before initiating the training program at Tuskegee Institute, there was great skepticism by white decision makers, including the first lady, Eleanor Roosevelt, about whether blacks were mentally capable of flying airplanes. This generally held belief was dispelled when an African-American pilot named Charles Alfred "Chief" Anderson flew over the Alabama college campus with the first lady as a passenger. (At that time, Anderson was the only black person who had passed the test for a commerical pilot's license from the Civil Aeronautics Administration.) They returned half an hour later and Mrs. Roosevelt was quick to acknowledge Anderson's ability as a pilot.

Between 1942 and 1946, 926 African-American pilots graduated from this training school. During World War II, 450 of the Tuskeegee Airmen, led by an African-American colonel named Benjamin O. Davis Jr., actually flew combat missions overseas. The segregated African-American pilots first served as a pursuit squadron in North Africa and Sicily. Some of the Tuskegee Airmen were later part of a fighter group that helped ruin the operations of the Italian railroad, destroyed hundreds of vehicles, and harassed German and Italian coastal surveillance outposts. Others, as fighter pilots protecting B-17 bombers with the 15th Army Air Group in Italy, managed to achieve devastating results in bombings over Germany, Czechoslovakia, and the Balkans. During the war, 66 black pilots were killed and 32 were captured.

Benjamin O. Davis Jr. was eventually promoted to the rank of brigadier general, the first black man to earn this rank in the U.S. Air Force. For his contributions as an outstanding military leader, Davis was posthumously elevated to the stature of four-star general by President Clinton in 1998.

The Tuskegee Airmen's distinguished reputation during World War II was based in part on their practice of pairing up fighter and bomber planes before going out on search and destroy missions. For this reason, none of their planes were shot down by the enemy fighters during bombing raids. This flying unit's other significant contribution to military history came when many of its members decided to remain active in what became the U.S. Air Force after the war ended and the armed forces became integrated.

African-American cadets line up for review in 1942 at what was then called The Basic and Advanced Flying School for Negro Air Corps Cadets. These Tuskegee Airmen broke the color barrier when they became the first black military pilots in the United States.

AFRICAN AMERICANS AND THE FILM INDUSTRY

With the success of Spike Lee's 1986 film *She's Gotta Have It*, it seemed that new chances were opening up for African-American actors. However, in large part, opportunities for black actors were the result of efforts by independent film-makers, such as Lee, who created and distributed their work often completely outside of the mainstream Hollywood studio system. Even at the dawn of a new millennium, there are still relatively few blacks and other minorities working in the film industry studio system; minority women are conspicuously absent.

These problems are nothing new: African Americans have been discriminated against in Hollywood, as in all facets of American life. There have been a few notable exceptions: the career of an independent black filmmaker named Oliver Micheaux spanned the 1920s, 1930s, and 1940s, and black actors such as Stepin Fetchit (the first black actor to receive star billing), Hattie McDaniel (the first African American to win an Oscar), and Bill "Bojangles" Robinson were able to break the color line fairly early in the history of film. Nevertheless, these talented entertainers were often relegated to stereotypical roles. Parts for blacks in films were written to appeal to a white audience, not to portray blacks as they view themselves; as a result these roles were caricatures, rather than characters.

Even when complex roles were available for black characters, in some cases these parts were filled by white actresses. In *Imitation of Life* (1934), Fredi Washington played a light-skinned African-American woman who passes for white. *Pinky*, directed by Elia Kazan in 1949, also features a white actress, Jeanne Crain, who plays a light-skinned black woman.

In the 1950s and early 1960s, an African American named Sidney Poitier began to portray more realistic characters. In films like *Blackboard Jungle* (1955), *Edge of the City* (1957), and *A Raisin in the Sun* (1961), Poitier portrayed African Americans with depth and feeling. However, other than Poitier and another popular black film star, Harry Belafonte, there were few successful African Americans in Hollywood during the decades following World War II.

By the late 1960s, however, African-American movements for civil rights and empowerment were in full swing. Pressure from civil-rights leaders, along with declining ticket sales due to the popularity of television, led the heads of the Hollywood studios to begin making films targeted at black audiences.

In 1969, Gordon Parks Sr. became the first black director of a major studio film, *The Learning Tree*, for Warner Brothers Studios. "I had fourteen or fifteen [black] people behind the camera for the first time in the history of films," Parks later recalled. "There was a black director. The producer was black. The scoring was done by a black man. The third cameraman for the first time was a black man. . . . The minute [Kenny Hyman of Warner Brothers] did it, everybody felt "well, it's happened. We better open up now."

The next year, a filmmaker named Melvin Van Peebles raised enough money to direct and produce *Sweet Sweetback's Baad Asssss Song*. Van Peebles's 1971 film, which he wrote and also starred in, is about a black man who is protected by others in the black community as he tries to elude police. The movie single-handedly "changed the course of African-American film production and the depiction of African Americans on screen," wrote Jesse Algeron Rhines in her 1996 book *Black Film/White Money*. The success of *Sweetback*, along with two contemporary movies, *Shaft* (1971, directed by Parks) and *Superfly* (1972, directed by Parks's son Gordon Jr.), ushered in the era of "blaxploitation" films. The term, coined by the industry publication *Variety*, usually refers to films portraying blacks as antiheroes—protagonists who lack admirable or heroic characters. However, unlike *Sweetback*, *Shaft*, and *Superfly*, most of these "blaxploitation" films were written, directed, and distributed by whites, who were merely exploiting the audience's interest in the subject.

Despite the increased exposure for black actors and actresses, blaxploitation films still represented a white view of blacks—albeit a view that was, perhaps because of its very extremism, popular with young black filmgoers. The roles for black men in blaxploitation films were just as limiting as stereotyped roles in earlier movies.

But even during the genre's heyday in the 1970s, other filmmakers were producing more genuine films for black audiences: Belafonte, Bill Cosby, Ossie Davis, and others such as the black-owned distribution companies TAM and Cinematics International. Sidney Poitier, too, was still a powerful influence in "white" Hollywood. These men continued to produce and direct films that

In 1969 Gordon Parks Sr. became the first black director of a major Hollywood film, The Learning Tree. Parks also produced the film, wrote the screenplay from his novel, and composed the musical score. His son, Gordon Parks Jr. (left), worked as a still photographer on the set.

portrayed blacks in a more realistic way.

In the 1980s and 1990s, a new crop of independent filmmakers began to appear on the Hollywood scene. The first, and one of the most influential, was Spike Lee, who followed *She's Gotta Have It* with hits like *Do the Right Thing* (1989), *Mo' Better Blues* (1990), and *Jungle Fever* (1991), as well as the epic *Malcom X* (1992). In 1991, 23-year-old John Singleton emerged with *Boyz N the Hood*; he followed this hit with *Poetic Justice* (1993) and *Higher Learning* (1995). Others included Robert Townsend (*Hollywood Shuffle*, 1987; *Meteor Man*, 1993) and Keenan Ivory Wayans (*I'm Gonna Git You Sucka*, a spoof of blaxploitation films, 1988).

Unlike these independents, an actor named Forest Whittaker started his directing career working with major Hollywood studios. The first film he directed, 1995's *Waiting to Exhale*, was based on the novel by Terry McMillan about the friendship of four black women. The movie was a smash hit. In 1998, Whittaker directed his second film, *Hope Floats*. Unlike *Waiting to Exhale* and other movies made by black filmmakers, *Hope Floats* featured an all-white cast. Perhaps in the future a black director whose movie tells a white person's story will not be so uncommon.

FURTHER READING

Crowe, Cameron. *Conversations With Wilder*. New York: Knopf, 1999.

Falk, Quentin. *Anthony Hopkins: The Authorized Biography*. Northampton, MA: Interlink Publishing, 1994.

Hardy, James Earl. *Spike Lee*. Philadelphia: Chelsea House, 1996.

Hill, Anne. *Denzel Washington*. Philadelphia: Chelsea House, 1999.

McCollum, Brian. "Like His Actor Son, Cuba Sr. Enjoys Star Status." *The Detroit Free Press* (5 June 1998): E-1.

Osborne, Robert. *70 Years of the Oscar: The Official History of the Academy Awards*. New York: Abbeville Press, 1999.

Powell, Phelan. *Tom Cruise*. Philadelphia: Chelsea House, 1999.

INDEX

PICTURE CREDITS

───── ❧ ─────

PAULA EDELSON is a freelance writer and journalist. She lives with her husband and two sons in Durham, North Carolina. Her other books for Chelsea House include *Superstars of Men's Tennis* (1998) and *Superstars of Men's Swimming and Diving* (1998).

NATHAN IRVIN HUGGINS, one of America's leading scholars in the field of black studies, helped select the titles for the BLACK AMERICANS OF ACHIEVEMENT series, for which he also served as senior consulting editor. He was the W. E. B. DuBois Professor of History and Afro-American Studies at Harvard University and the director of the W. E. B. DuBois Institute for Afro-American Research at Harvard. He received his doctorate from Harvard in 1962 and returned there as professor in 1980 after teaching at Columbia University, the University of Massachusetts, Lake Forest College, and the California State University, Long Beach. He was the author of four books and dozens of articles, including *Black Odyssey: The Afro-American Ordeal in Slavery*, *The Harlem Renaissance*, and *Slave and Citizen: The Life of Frederick Douglass*, and was associated with the Children's Television Workshop, National Public Radio, the Boston Athenaeum, the Museum of Afro-American History, the Howard Thurman Educational Trust, and Upward Bound. Professor Huggins died in 1989, at the age of 62, in Cambridge, Massachusetts.

19.95

- - B Gooding E
Edelson, Paula.
Cuba Gooding Jr.